FRANCIS FRITH'S
A JOURNEY AROUND ENGLAND

Compiled by Shelley Tolcher and Julia Skinner
Introduction by Julia Skinner

First published in the United Kingdom in 2004 by
Frith Book Company Ltd

Hardback Edition 2004
ISBN 1-85937-788-2

British Library Cataloguing in Publication Data

Francis Frith's A Journey Around England
Compiled by Shelley Tolcher and Julia Skinner

Frith Book Company Ltd
Frith's Barn, Teffont,
Salisbury, Wiltshire SP3 5QP
Tel: +44 (0) 1722 716 376
Email: info@francisfrith.co.uk
www.francisfrith.co.uk

Printed and bound in Spain

The colour-tinting is for illustrative purposes only, and is not intended to be historically accurate

AS WITH ANY HISTORICAL DATABASE THE FRITH ARCHIVE IS CONSTANTLY BEING CORRECTED AND IMPROVED
AND THE PUBLISHERS WOULD WELCOME INFORMATION ON OMISSIONS OR INACCURACIES

CONTENTS

A JOURNEY AROUND ENGLAND

introduction

THE EARLIEST FORMS of roads and tracks are believed to have been paths taken by man the hunter, following the trails of wild animals. When early trade systems developed, from the Neolithic period onwards, the traders travelled over long-distance routes that probably followed either watersheds, or the raised ground above marshy areas or river basins, or the high ground above the heavily forested landscape. These ancient routes are known nowadays by names such as the Ridgeway and the Icknield Way, which followed the tops or sides of valleys. The most important of these routes were the Harroway (from Dover to Cornwall), the Ridgeway (from the Goring Gap to the important Neolithic area of Salisbury Plain), the Icknield Way (a northerly extension of the Ridgeway), and part of what was later known as the Pilgrim's Way, which ran along the North Downs from Winchester to Canterbury. Amongst the goods that the traders would have carried were probably salt, tin, copper, and flint tools. Items made of flint originating from all over Europe have been found throughout the British Isles, as well as those made of flint from the Neolithic flint mines known as Grime's Graves near Thetford in Norfolk.

During the period of Roman administration at least 10,000 miles (16,000km) of roads were built in England, mainly to give easy access to the garrison towns placed strategically throughout the country. The Roman roads radiated out from Londinium, the area near present-day London Bridge. Certain sections of these roads appear to have been constructed on what were once prehistoric tracks, showing a continuity of use which in some cases continues to this day, since many modern roads were built over the Roman routes. The imperial roads were so well made that many of them were still in use during the medieval period; King Edward the Confessor passed laws to ensure that the principal Roman routes of Watling Street, the Fosse Way, Hikenith (the Icknield Way) and Ermine Street were kept clear from sea to sea.

In the Anglo-Saxon and early medieval period, roads,

paths and tracks were mainly used by travellers on foot or horse-back, or by trains of pack-horses; heavier goods were probably transported for the most part by river or on 'sledges', as wheeled traffic was not a practical option on wet or muddy ground. Early names reflect the different uses of these routes. Portways were lanes which led to a town or market ('port' meant 'market', and these lanes became known as 'port straets'); herepaths were routes taken by armies; corpse-paths were the paths along which the dead were carried to burial at remote churches, especially in the north of England; and the Anglo-Saxon 'holloways' are often still known as 'green lanes'. There were also important Anglo-Saxon routes associated with the salt trade, known variously as 'sealt path', 'sealstraet' and 'sealtrod'.

The administrative systems of the Middle Ages depended on the king and his officials being able constantly to move around the country to collect taxes, check on their estates, administer justice, and generally show themselves to their subjects as a means of enforcing their rule and prestige. The early records show that the kings were always travelling: King John, for example, only spent one month of his entire reign without a move, changing households, on average, over thirteen times each month during his reign - and of course when the king moved, so did his household and retinue. The importance of keeping the roads in good repair was recognised by Henry I, who forbade any encroachment on the roads under a penalty of one hundred shillings. King Stephen strengthened the laws when in 1140 he ordered the lords of the manor to keep the highways open. Gridlock was also obviously a problem for the early medieval traveller, since various laws were passed stating that major roads were to be sufficiently wide for two wagons to be able to pass each other, for two oxherds to be able to make their goads touch across them, and for 16 armed knights to be able to ride side by side along them.

As with the Roman roads, medieval kings also ordered roads to be built and maintained for military purposes; for

4

instance, in 1278 Edward I ordered the roads and passes into parts of north Wales to be enlarged and widened as part of his campaigns against the Welsh. The building of castles and ecclesiastical centres such as churches, cathedrals, abbeys and monasteries in the Middle Ages also created a need for better roads to enable movement of stone, but the major influence on roads and transport in medieval times was the growth of trade and the development of markets. The population of England increased markedly in the early Middle Ages (until halted by the Black Death of 1348-49), which created a growing demand for that most basic of human needs - food. The increased demand for fresh, perishable produce can be seen in a proliferation of Royal Charters in the 13th and 14th centuries establishing the right of towns to hold a market; this coincided with the growth of the wool and cloth industry, whose economic importance to the history of England cannot be overstated. Town populations were swelled by workers in the cloth trade and associated industries, and the towns themselves developed into important centres as their markets and industries became more established. All transport routes were now of vital importance to the economic and social fabric of the country, whether by road, river, passes, fords, and river- and sea-ports; the growth of trade led to more wheeled traffic, which made roads rutted and difficult to use. The building and maintaining of roads and bridges was essential to the success of the market towns and their local industries and hinterland, and was often undertaken by the Church. After the Dissolution of the Monasteries in the 16th century, the condition of the roads deteriorated; the Highway Act of 1555 officially made the Church no longer responsible for the maintenance of roads, but laid the burden onto the local parishes through 'voluntary' forced labour of 4 (later 6) days a year, in recognition of the importance of maintaining the transport system in good condition.

These early roads must have been busy and colourful, thronged with travellers from all walks of life, from royal parties, officials and messengers, soldiers, merchants with carts full of wool and cloth, and farmers with their farm produce, to itinerant pedlars, bear-men, medieval showmen, 'sturdy beggars' and the destitute. Many of the travellers would have been associated with the Church, such as wandering friars, preachers, pardoners and, of course, pilgrims, illustrating some of the most famous lines in English literature:

'Than longen folk to goon on pilgrimages …
And specially from every shires ende
Of Engelond to Caunterbury they wende …'
('The Canterbury Tales', Geoffrey Chaucer, written c1400).

Travel in these times was not without its dangers, however, as can be seen from the legislation of the period. King Edward I's Trench Act of 1285 ordered that where a road ran through a wood the trees were to be cut back to a width of 60 feet on either side of the King's Way; in other words, the Act required the clearing of a space on each side of more than the length of a bow-shot, preventing outlaws from firing arrows from cover close to the road. Similarly, the Statute of Winchester of 1293 decreed that all highways from one market town to another were to be enlarged so that 'there is no dyke or bush within 200 feet on either side'. Further legislation in 1536 caused bridges to have parapets of three feet or more in height, to deter robbers. Travel was such a dangerous and precarious business that many town bridges had chapels built on them to enable travellers to give thanks after a safe journey, or to ask for a blessing before starting out - examples to be seen in this book are at Bradford-on-Avon, and Elvet Bridge at Durham. Even if the lucky traveller escaped the attentions of outlaws and robbers, the road itself could still claim its victim: there is a sad tale from 1499 of a glover from Leighton Buzzard who fell into a pit in the road whilst riding home from Aylesbury market in the dark. The pit had been dug earlier by servants of a local miller who had needed clay to repair his mill; they left a hole in the road ten feet wide and eight feet deep, which soon filled with water from the winter rains. The unfortunate glover and his horse were both drowned.

In 1656, during the reign of Charles II, highway rates were introduced to keep the roads maintained in good repair, and in 1663 the first turnpike (toll-paying) road was introduced into England; but one of the major influences on transport and roads was again the growth of the population, especially that of London, which required feeding. The period between 1750-1850 was the era of long-distance droving: livestock were moved 'on the hoof' to fattening fields and markets along drove roads, or 'driftways'. Cattle droves would consist of approximately 200 head of cattle; Welsh drovers had animals entrusted to them by their owners, but Scottish drovers usually purchased the animals themselves before setting out for the markets of the

Midlands or London. The scale of droving was huge - it has been estimated that in the 1700s, around 600,000 sheep were driven into Smithfield market each year. Turkeys and geese from East Anglia were also 'driven', their feet protected from the road by a mixture of tar, sand and sawdust, to the famous Goose Fairs at Nottingham and Tavistock. The droving process was slow, and time had to be allowed at the end of the journey for the animals to rest and put on weight before market; geese driven to the Leadenhall Market in London would set out from East Anglia in August, but would not arrive in London until the end of October. Pigs were also driven along hogways, particularly from Wales to Bristol, and from Cornwall to London.

In the late 18th century the Industrial Revolution completely changed the way in which raw materials and finished goods were moved around the country. Before industrialisation the main transport system was a train of 40 or 50 pack-horses, with jingling bells on their harness to warn of their approach as they clattered along the stone-slabbed hard surface of their narrow pack-horse trails and over the picturesque pack-horse bridges found all over the country, often with a ford alongside for heavier carts and wagons. The manufactories and mills of the Industrial Revolution depended on water and vast supplies of coal for their power, and so they were usually sited near rivers, which were then used to transport raw materials and finished goods; later the canal system was developed around the industrialised areas and linking them, which allowed more extensive and direct movement of materials and goods in and out. At the peak of the canal age there were 4,000 miles of inland waterways - the canal water was described as ' black as the Styx and absolutely pestiferous.'

The important development in the road systems was turnpiking, whereby a toll-road was set up by a group of investors, and part of the income was used to keep the road clear and in good repair from one market town to another. By 1821 over 18,000 miles (29,000km) of English roads had been turnpiked. These roads were of major importance in improving the transport of merchandise, but they also allowed greater movement of people - the development of the turnpike roads opened up the coaching era. Communications also improved dramatically. News could now travel swiftly all around the country, as well as letters, parcels and consumer goods. Travel was still most uncomfortable, but that owed as much to the design of the coaches and carriages as to the rutted state of the roads. However, many roads were much improved by the methods of John McAdam (1756-1836), whose three-layered system of road-building forms the basis of modern road construction today, now refined by the addition of tar on the surface, which binds the stone chippings together. Travellers on these roads still ran the risk of danger, and the chance of meeting 'gentlemen of the road', as areas such as Bagshot Heath were notorious haunts of highwaymen. Travel could also still be difficult in bad weather, as this quote from 'A Tale of Two Cities' by Charles Dickens (1859) illustrates:

'He walked up hill in the mire by the side of the mail, as the rest of the passengers did; not because they had the least relish for walking exercise, under the circumstances, but because the hill, and the harness, and the mud, and the mail, were all so heavy, that the horses had already come to a stop ...'

The coaching trade was the making of many towns that lay on the main coaching routes. For example, it has been estimated that at the height of the coaching era up to 500 coaches crossed the bridge at Maidenhead every day. Inns provided food, accommodation and fresh horses for travellers, but a host of ancillary trades and businesses in the towns also benefited from the coaching custom. By 1836 around 700 mail coaches and 3,300 passenger coaches were in regular operation around the country.

The state of the roads in the 19th century was much improved by the effects of the Highway Act of 1835, which established parish and district surveyors and highway boards, and the 1875 Public Health Act, which created Urban Sanitary Districts and improved road and street conditions in towns. However, by this time another development had taken place, which had a huge impact on every aspect of life in England: the coming of the railways. The railway system was originally envisaged as a freight-carrying operation, with passenger services only operating as a sideline. Between 1825 and 1835 500 miles of track had been laid, but then 'railway mania' took hold: by 1843 there were 2,036 miles of track in use, and a further 8,730 miles had been sanctioned by 1847. Despite some initial fears about the speed of the trains being dangerous to the health of passengers, the Victorians took to the railways with gusto, following the enthusiastic example of their Queen. By 1855 all the great cities of the country had been linked,

INTRODUCTION

and some new towns had appeared on the map, such as Crewe, which had not even been present as a place name in the 1841 census. The railway system revolutionised the distribution of consumer goods, perishable products, and manufactured items, as well as giving the population a freedom of movement never before experienced. The novelist William Thackeray complained: 'We who lived before railways and survive out of the ancient world are like Father Noah and his family out of the Ark.'

The railway brought success or ruin to the towns and villages of England, relative to their dependence on the coaching trade or their proximity to the new lines. Those towns that were on coaching routes but not reached by the railway line suffered, as the coaching trade declined dramatically against competition from the trains. Other small villages and towns experienced an economic boom if they were on the rail system, or developed rapidly as desirable locations for homes if the railway allowed easy and quick access to places of work. The railway companies eventually realised the potential of passenger travel. Between 1849 and 1870 the number of first- and second-class passengers increased by four times, and the number of third-class passengers increased by six times. An Act of Parliament of 1844 required the railway companies to run at least one train every weekday at a reduced fare, which encouraged all levels of society to use the trains. This move was supported by Thomas Cook, founder of the travel agency, who declared 'We must have railways for the millions', and the first excursion train ran to Brighton in 1844. The Bank Holiday Act of 1871 helped develop seaside holiday resorts, and the railway system was an important factor in the growth of the tourist industry generally, throughout the whole country.

It was precisely at this time that the photographer Francis Frith began his project to photograph every city, town and village in Britain. For the next thirty years he travelled around the country producing photographs of seaside resorts, beauty spots and street scenes that were bought by millions as reminders of their holidays and days out. After Frith's death in 1898 the business was continued by his sons, who expanded the photograph collection and then began to produce the views as postcards. These beautiful photographs are now reproduced as prints by The Francis Frith Collection, and are being seen by a new generation as part of a continuing programme of local history publications.

Our aim in this book is, wherever possible, to show some of the best and oldest views of towns and villages around England, to see the country as it appeared to Francis Frith and his sons, set against Victorian maps showing the counties as they were at that time. Several points have been particularly noticeable to us whilst compiling this collection: the historical importance of markets and the wool and cloth trade to so many towns around the country; the number of towns which were destroyed by fire, confirming how vulnerable closely-packed thatched and timber-framed buildings were in the past; the economic importance of transport and communications to the development of a town, and the enormous impact of the coaching routes and railways; and how times have changed, since we now demand that our modern towns are bypassed by traffic and motorways - what has historically been the life-blood of a town is now seen as the kiss of death. It could be said that these photographs show a nostalgic view of the past, but these are actual scenes, not a film set. Some idea of the reality of the past can be gained by a comment about Bristol: for decades a major problem facing the Bristol Health Board was how to combat the daily stench during the summer months created by tons of horse-droppings in the streets. An early experiment using water carts to damp down the streets found that it took 7,000 gallons to water one mile of street of 18 feet in width at a cost of 8s 4d per mile: the result of the 1861 experiment found that Bristol would need 83 carts to water the streets twice a day. However, this pungent view of the past can be balanced against another, equally authentic, comment by the American writer Henry James, whilst visiting Much Wenlock in Shropshire: 'an ancient little town ... with no great din of vehicles ... a dozen 'publics', with tidy whitewashed cottages ... and little girls bobbing curtsies in the street.'

This book shows the England that we have now lost to the motorcar, England at work and play, wealthy and poor, stylish or ragged. Real people pass through its pages: people whose names we do not know, captured for a moment at the edge of a photograph before they move out of frame and back into their lives.

cornwall

Cornwall is encircled by water, surrounded by the sea on three sides and separated from the rest of England by the River Tamar. In this beautiful but harsh landscape Cornish people made their living in perilous ways: from the sea as fishermen, sailors, smugglers or wreckers, and from the land in farming and the mineral and china clay industries. The decline of the tin and copper mines led to Cornishmen emigrating in search of mining work - known as 'Cousin Jacks' the saying was that you could find a Cornishman at the bottom of any hole in the world.

During the early 19th century any extension of the railway to the far west of England had been piecemeal. Mineral railways were part of Cornwall's mining industry from the earliest years of the century, but it was only in the 1850s that a railway line was opened between Penzance and Truro. By 1849 trains were running between London and Plymouth. Brunel's railway bridge over the Tamar was opened in 1859, and now the last great obstacle to expansion westwards was overcome.

This rail link with London was of huge value: it meant that perishable products such as fish from the Cornish seas and early flowers and potatoes from farms could be transported to major markets within a day. The traffic was two-way, but the return traffic was in human form: the fast developing tourist industry brought more and more visitors to the far west, to the irresistible attraction of Lands End and to the new leisure activity of sea bathing.

TRURO, BOSCAWEN STREET 1912 64732

The bustling centre of Truro is paved with granite setts. Formerly at the heart of a mining district, Truro's great glory is its cathedral, built by J L Pearson between 1880 and 1909 in the Early English style. The central tower rises 250 feet into the sky, and was conceived as a memorial to Queen Victoria.

PENZANCE, THE PROMENADE 1906 56508

Despite the relative shelter offered by Mounts Bay, winter storms can sometimes be ferocious. A particularly bad one on 7 October 1880 destroyed the promenade and also killed seven men on the Mousehole boat 'Jane'. Penzance was 'a place of good business, well built and populous, having a good trade and a great many ships belonging to it', according to Daniel Defoe, when he visited in the 17th century. Today the ships are rather less numerous - the Isles of Scilly boat 'Scillonian' is the only vessel of any size to operate from the harbour.

PENRYN, A STREET 1890 27649

Penryn is an interesting town at the head of a tidal creek off Falmouth harbour, and was a port long before being overtaken by Falmouth.

FALMOUTH, THE MARKET STRAND 1890 24208

The three passenger steamers alongside the quay are, from left to right, the 'New Resolute', the 'Wotton' and probably the 'St Mawes Castle'. Market Strand Quay was later extended in 1905 to become the Prince of Wales Pier, which is still used for ferry services.

CORNWALL

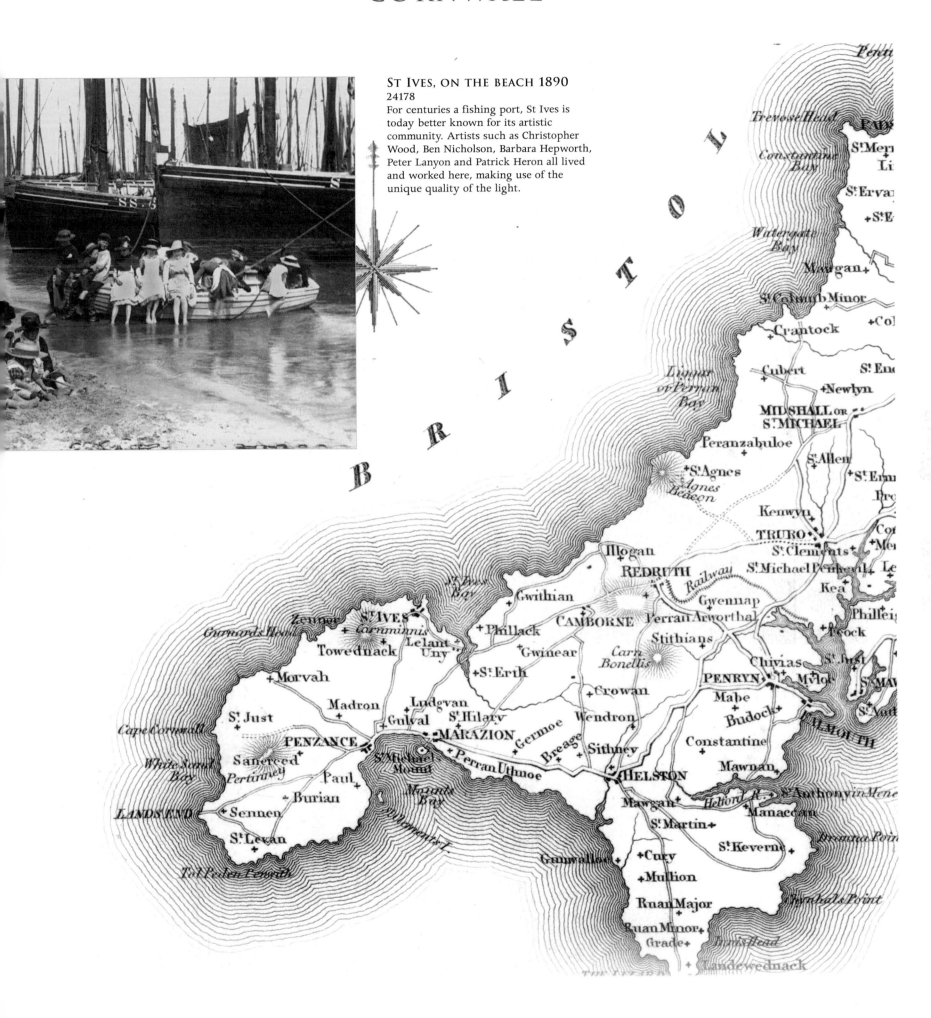

St Ives, on the beach 1890
24178
For centuries a fishing port, St Ives is today better known for its artistic community. Artists such as Christopher Wood, Ben Nicholson, Barbara Hepworth, Peter Lanyon and Patrick Heron all lived and worked here, making use of the unique quality of the light.

**ST AUSTELL
CHARLESTOWN HARBOUR 1912** 64784
Charlestown was developed by Sir Charles Rashleigh at the
beginning of the 19th century for exporting china clay
and other minerals.

TINTAGEL, KING ARTHUR'S CASTLE 1894 33595A
Despite the Arthurian legends attached to Tintagel, it seems
doubtful that Camelot was actually here. There is no denying
the power of the remains of the medieval castle on the 270ft-
high island, however - or their pulling power for visitors.

**PADSTOW, MARKET PLACE
1906** 56268
The harbour at Padstow
originally belonged to Bodmin
Priory and has had many
celebrated visitors, none more
so, perhaps, than Sir Walter
Raleigh, who used it frequently
when he was Lord Warden of the
Stannaries in the 16th century.
Although it is sheltered the
estuary has claimed many ships.
The famous Doom Bar (so famous
it even has a beer named after
it!) extends from the west shore
for nearly half a mile; in a big
swell and falling tide it becomes
a vicious mass of white water.
Along the southern shore of the
estuary runs the branch line
from Wadebridge. The first train
ran on 23 March 1899. The last
train was on 28 January 1967,
and the line is now the Camel
Trail, a superb cycleway.

BODMIN, FORE STREET 1906 56279
The origins of Bodmin date back to Norman times. The 15th-century parish church, dedicated to
St Petroc, is the largest in Cornwall. The county gaol on the northern edge of the town was used
for the safekeeping of the Domesday Book and the Crown Jewels during the First World War.

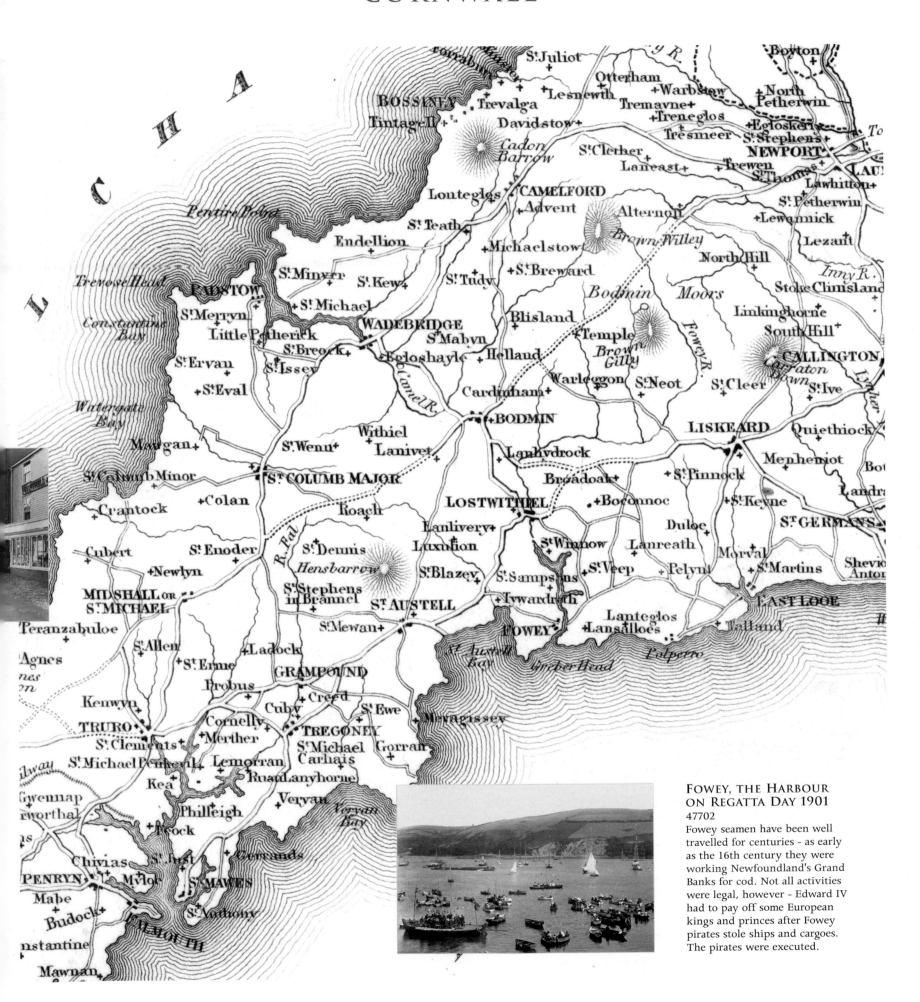

FOWEY, THE HARBOUR ON REGATTA DAY 1901
47702
Fowey seamen have been well travelled for centuries - as early as the 16th century they were working Newfoundland's Grand Banks for cod. Not all activities were legal, however - Edward IV had to pay off some European kings and princes after Fowey pirates stole ships and cargoes. The pirates were executed.

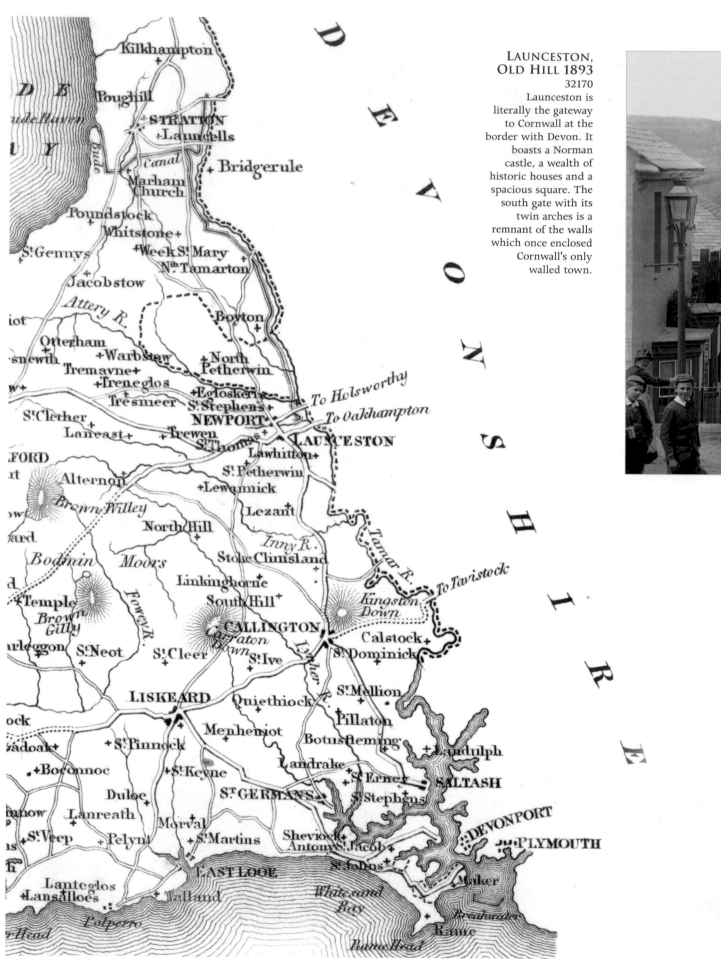

Launceston is literally the gateway to Cornwall at the border with Devon. It boasts a Norman castle, a wealth of historic houses and a spacious square. The south gate with its twin arches is a remnant of the walls which once enclosed Cornwall's only walled town.

CORNWALL

KILKHAMPTON, THE VILLAGE 1910 62406
This hilltop village, at the head of the Coombe Valley, sits astride the main road between Bude and Barnstaple, which was once the pilgrim's route to St Michael's Mount.

POLPERRO, THE HARBOUR 1901 47794
Polperro's east facing harbour entrance, protected by twin quays, is sheltered from westerlies, but in 1824 a mighty easterly storm demolished the breakwaters and wrecked the fishing fleet. The pilchard fisheries of Cornwall were considered so important that an Admiralty edict of the 18th century stated that no pilchard men were to be press-ganged.

LISKEARD, FORE STREET 1906 56300
This distinguished market town reached the height of its prosperity when the copper mines, at the edges of the wild wastes of Bodmin at Caradon Hill, were working at full capacity. Great Western trains thundered through Liskeard bound for Penzance, carrying travellers to within ten miles of Land's End.

SALTASH, THE FERRY 1924 76023
For travellers to Cornwall, crossing the broad sweeping waters of the Tamar deepened the sensation that they were entering a foreign land. Some took the chugging chain ferry, and others rattled over Brunel's curious bridge in the carriages of the Great Western Railway, built in 1859.

devon

In 1837 less than a third of Devon's population lived in towns. The majority lived in the myriad villages, hamlets and farmsteads that dotted the landscape. A network of some 7,000 miles of what might loosely be termed roads linked these settlements, but only a fraction were suitable for travel at any sort of pace. The turnpike roads, usually administered by trusts, served the most important places, and made it possible to travel from London to Exeter in some twenty hours. On one occasion, in 1835, the 'Quicksilver' coach carrying the Devonport mail made the journey from London in just over twenty-one hours, a feat which must have tried the endurance of even the hardiest passenger.

Away from the turnpikes, however, travel was a very different matter. The horse and cart, or good old Shanks pony, were the only options open to many Devonians, although those living on estuaries or by the sea might use a ferry or a trading schooner. For the most part people stayed where they were, save for a weekly trip to the nearest market, and perhaps, for the few, a visit to the annual fair in one of the big towns.

By the 1840s Devon stood on the threshold of a transport revolution. The name of the man who would bring it about was unknown to many, but by the time of his untimely death in 1859 Isambard Kingdom Brunel had become a national hero. There were countless others involved, of course - financiers, politicians, lawyers - and indeed there were other engineers the equal of Brunel in skill; but none had the grand vision (or the flair for publicity) of the little man with the stovepipe hat and side whiskers. The Bristol and Exeter railway was the first to cross the border, reaching the county's capital in 1844 and reducing the journey time from London to a mere five hours. Over the next five years Brunel pushed the South Devon Railway through to Plymouth and during the following sixty years there was a constant expansion of the network.

ILFRACOMBE, CAPSTONE HILL AND PARADE 1911
63901
Ilfracombe was a market town until the Napoleonic Wars closed the Continent to visitors, and tourists began to explore the British Isles instead. Paddle steamers were a major feature of the town's success as a resort, and one, the 'Waverley', still visits for a few weeks each summer.

PLYMOUTH, THE BARBICAN 1890 22474
Crammed onto a broad peninsula that is delineated by rivers to the east and west, and blocked by hills to the north and the sea to the south, it is remarkable how Plymouth manages to squeeze 250,000 people into perhaps seven or eight square miles. Pressure for living space has profoundly altered the landscape of Plymouth over the centuries. Down in the valleys, things are very different from how they would have been in the time of Sir Francis Drake. Then, the city centre and the Hoe were within a mile of being an island, for tidal creeks reached as far as Pennycomequick and Lipson Vale. The lower part of St Jude's was a tidal mudflat, Marsh Mills was just that - a marsh, and the Devonport shore was damp and uninhabited. Hills such as the ones that are now occupied by Mount Gould, Mannamead and North Hill would have been open spaces, grazed by cattle and sheep, and travel out of the city was possible only via ford or ferry.

APPLEDORE, THE RICHMOND
DOCK 1923 75148
The busy little port of Appledore is now home to just a few fishing boats. The quay has been straightened and raised, but the houses behind are substantially unchanged. Inevitably the type of boat that ties up today has changed somewhat.

BARNSTAPLE,
HIGH STREET 1903 49620
Barnstaple is situated at the head of the Taw estuary and is North Devon's largest town. It has a long commercial history, and was once the home of many prosperous textile merchants. Like Bideford, it gets its name from the location of an ancient ford, which was once marked by a staple, or post.

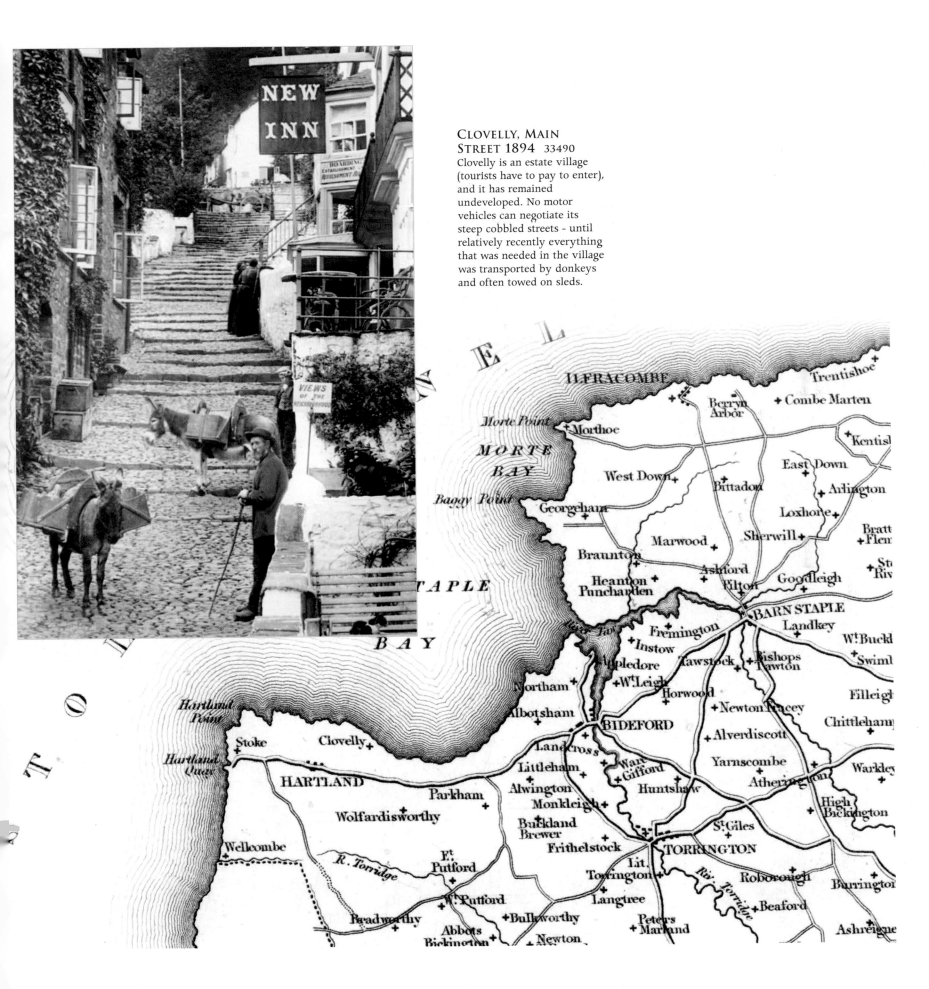

CLOVELLY, MAIN STREET 1894 33490
Clovelly is an estate village (tourists have to pay to enter), and it has remained undeveloped. No motor vehicles can negotiate its steep cobbled streets - until relatively recently everything that was needed in the village was transported by donkeys and often towed on sleds.

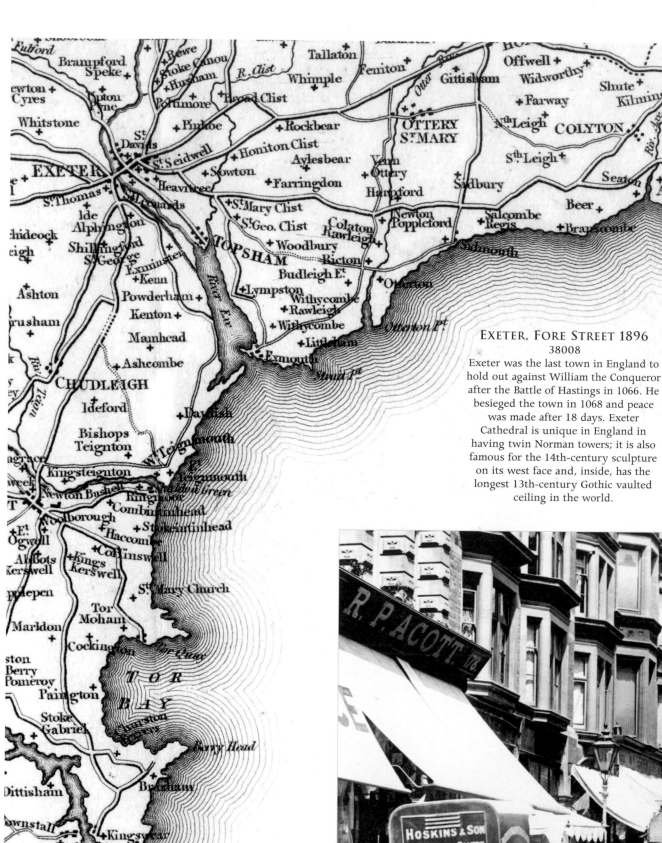

EXETER, FORE STREET 1896
38008
Exeter was the last town in England to hold out against William the Conqueror after the Battle of Hastings in 1066. He besieged the town in 1068 and peace was made after 18 days. Exeter Cathedral is unique in England in having twin Norman towers; it is also famous for the 14th-century sculpture on its west face and, inside, has the longest 13th-century Gothic vaulted ceiling in the world.

DEVON

TEIGNMOUTH, FROM THE PIER 1903 49560
Teignmouth has been a busy port for centuries, shipping the local clay and also the granite that built the original London Bridge from Swell Tor quarries. It became a resort in the late 18th and early 19th centuries. The poet John Keats wrote his epic poem 'Endymion' here.

SIDMOUTH, FORE STREET 1904 52071
Sidmouth is documented as Sedemuda in the Domesday book. It lies at the base of a beautiful valley, protected from the elements by sandstone cliffs, where the River Sid runs into the sea. There was once a harbour, but in the 15th century, after a particularly long spell of stormy weather, land fell from the cliffs, causing the harbour to be blocked up. Once a quiet fishing town, the architecture around Sidmouth features an array of different designs, eras and identities, and some 500 buildings are now officially 'listed'.

DARTMOUTH, NEW QUAY
1890 25289

Dartmouth was once one of England's greatest ports, exporting wool and cloth. In late Victorian times attendance at the annual Dartmouth regatta was highly chic and drew many wealthy participants and spectators. Queen Victoria much admired the town and its beautiful estuary, recording in her diary that '...the place is lovely, with its wooded rocks and church and castle at the entrance'.

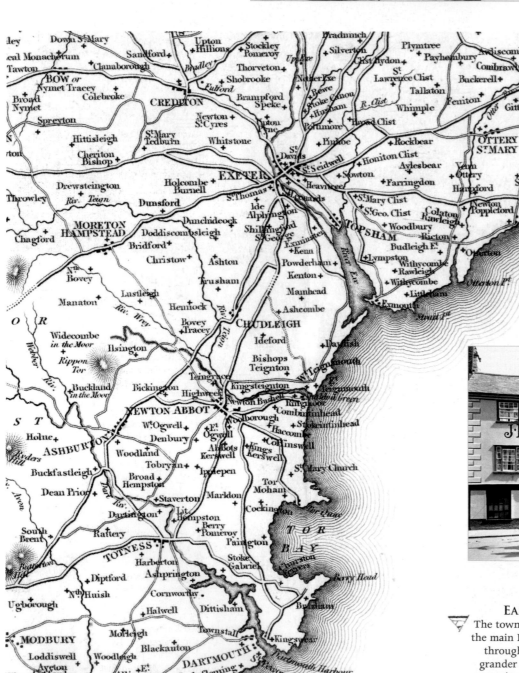

ASHBURTON,
EAST STREET AND BULL RING 1922 73181

The town lies just inside the Dartmoor National Park, alongside the main Exeter to Plymouth road. Once stagecoaches thundered through, forcing bystanders onto the narrow pavements. In grander and more prosperous days Ashburton was one of the region's strategic stannary towns. Mining finally came to a halt in the 19th century.

PAIGNTON, PRESTON SANDS 1918 68533

If Torquay always saw itself as rather upper-class, Paignton cheerfully catered for the hoi polloi. To this day, it is a candy floss and funny hats sort of a place: cheap and cheerful, very cheerful. Small changing tents were a feature of English seaside holiday towns until well after the last war.

TORQUAY, ANSTEY'S COVE 1896
38609

The Victorian development of Torquay, was definitely the province of the well-heeled, with sumptuous villas built along carefully contoured roads. The good climate and improved road and rail links made the town a very popular resort and a haven for the rich and famous.

NEWTON ABBOT, THE MARKET 1925
78550

Newton Abbot gained in importance in the 19th century by being a railway town. The Great Western Railway built a workshop here, and two main lines - to Plymouth and Torbay - divided just beyond the station. Most of the architecture is Victorian, including the fine Market Hall.

somerset

Somerset is a county of great beauty and variety in its roughly 70 miles from east to west and 30 miles from north to south. Its northern boundary is the Bristol Channel, and in the south it comes to within seven miles of the English Channel.

Sandwiched between the main body of England and the extremities of Devon and Cornwall, Somerset is a transition from the soft, mellow limestone hills that are such a feature of the heart of England to the wild, lonely moorland and rugged coasts that characterise the far west peninsula. Although not the largest of counties, it boasts a National Park in Exmoor and three designated Areas of Outstanding Beauty: the Mendip, Quantock and Blackdown Hills. Mention should also be made of Somerset's other great distinctive feature, the Levels, vast tracts of land barely above sea-level, often flooded, punctuated by island-like hills.

In the Middle Ages profits from Somerset's wool and cloth industries financed the raising of many elegant church towers and the foundation of monasteries and abbeys. Glastonbury Abbey, with its early Christian traditions and dubious King Arthur connection, drew crowds of pilgrims, the medieval equivalent of tourists. In the late 18th century Richard 'Beau' Nash made Bath stylish for the wealthy and fashionable. The city is now regarded as one of the finest architectural achievements of its age, and it remains one of the most popular destinations for visitors to Britain. By the Victorian period the popularity of sea-water bathing led to the development of seaside resorts such as Weston-super-Mare, Burnham-on-Sea and Minehead, aided by the arrival of the railway to bring in the holiday makers. Steam trains reached Weston in 1848, Burnham in 1858 and Minehead in 1874. Other visitors came to Somerset to thrill at Cheddar Gorge, and explore the caves at Cheddar and Wookey Hole.

TAUNTON, FORE STREET 1902 48723

The county town of Taunton lies at the very heart of Somerset, with the Quantock and Brendon Hills and Exmoor to the west and the low-lying marshes of the Somerset Levels to the east. This ancient borough takes its name from the River Tone, which winds through the town. The two traditional industries of Taunton Deane were cloth production and agriculture. In a sense one was dependent upon the other, for wool provided the raw material for the cloth, not least the rough serge known as 'Taunton Cloth'. It was the riches from both of these trades that led to the construction of Taunton's finest buildings, not least its churches with their soaring towers.

SHEPTON MALLET, TOWN STREET 1899 44843
Five miles east of Wells in the eastern Mendips, Shepton Mallet was a prosperous wool manufacturing town, which declined when the Industrial Revolution got underway in the north of England. In the 19th century, various industries were established to replace the wool cloth ones; these included brewing, with the splendidly named Anglo-Bavarian Brewery being established near Commercial Road.

BRIDGWATER, THE BRIDGE 1902 48712
Bridgwater, a prosperous industrial and commercial town, has a fine historic core. Its architectural focus is the domed Market Hall and St Mary's Church with its tall spire emerging from a somewhat squat tower. Bridgwater was an important port, with railway docks and the terminus of the Taunton and Bridgwater Canal. Its well-known corrugated clay pantiles were widely used, shipped by barge and railway wagon.

TAUNTON, EAST STREET 1902 48724
In mid-Victorian times, old Taunton town began to change from its old medieval layout to much the street pattern we see today. In this great age of civic reconstruction, old churches were restored, in Taunton's case quite sympathetically, and new municipal buildings rose. Whole new roads were laid out, such as the aptly-named Corporation Street, and shops were founded. Railways brought new residents and visitors to Taunton, and modern industries were founded on the edge of the town.

BURNHAM-ON-SEA, THE BEACH 1913 65386
Burnham-on-Sea is in effect on the east side of the River Parrett's estuary.

SOMERSET

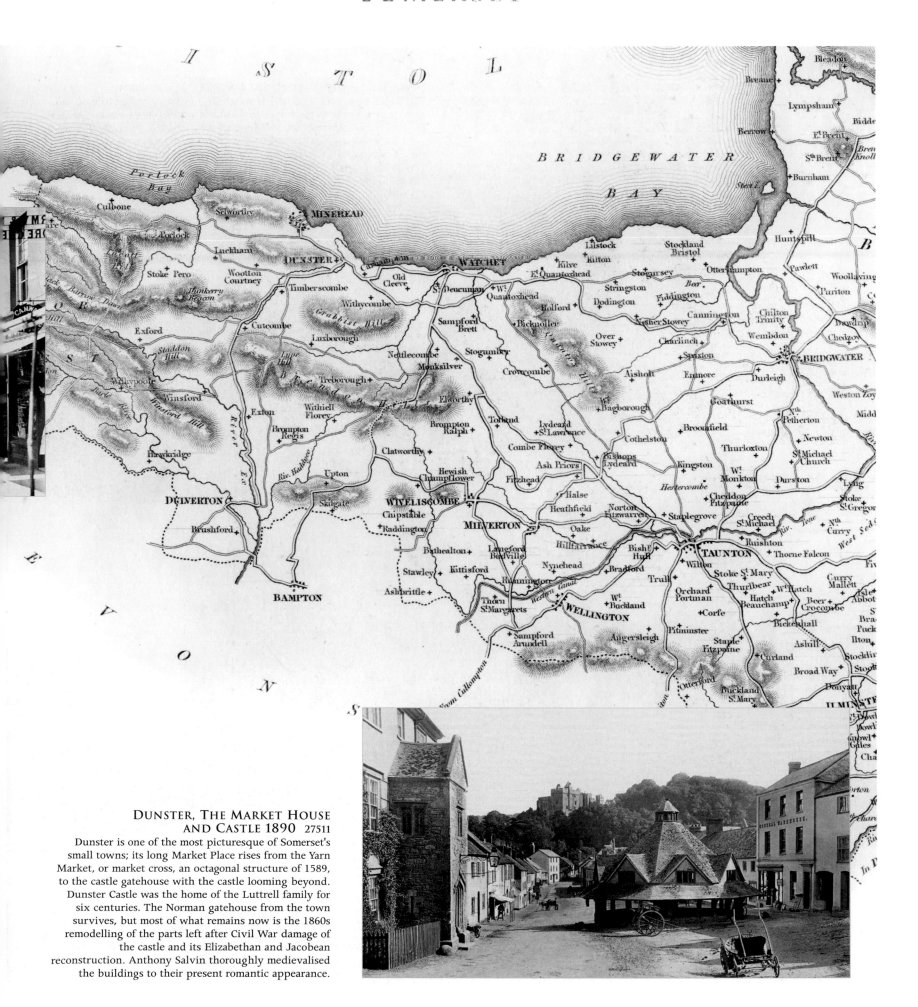

DUNSTER, THE MARKET HOUSE AND CASTLE 1890 27511

Dunster is one of the most picturesque of Somerset's small towns; its long Market Place rises from the Yarn Market, or market cross, an octagonal structure of 1589, to the castle gatehouse with the castle looming beyond. Dunster Castle was the home of the Luttrell family for six centuries. The Norman gatehouse from the town survives, but most of what remains now is the 1860s remodelling of the parts left after Civil War damage of the castle and its Elizabethan and Jacobean reconstruction. Anthony Salvin thoroughly medievalised the buildings to their present romantic appearance.

27

GLASTONBURY, THE TOR 1896 38382
Glastonbury, situated in eastern Somerset, is one of England's most historic smaller towns. It was a major centre of pilgrimage in the Middle Ages and still regarded by many as of mythic importance. The 'discovery' of King Arthur and Queen Guinevere's graves in the 12th century is today still a powerful draw. The town of Glastonbury had humble origins as the settlement that grew up outside the Abbey. Various servants of the Abbey and tradespeople who did business with the monks lived here. Gradually the town grew more important in its own right, acting as a market for the surrounding countryside, especially of course after Henry VIII's Dissolution of the Monasteries.

CHARD, THE OLD HOUSE, FORE STREET 1907 58766
Chard is a market town laid out in 1234 by Bishop Jocelyn of Wells. It grew into a prosperous wool town; in the 19th century cloth-making was replaced by lace-making and producing agricultural machinery.

FROME, THE OLDEST HOUSE 1907 58851
The town, built in oolitic limestone, is a most attractive one: its streets curve up and down hill picturesquely. Like Shepton Mallet and other southern cloth towns, it prospered until the woollen industry moved to Lancashire and Yorkshire's new mills after 1800 - thus in effect preserving the town for us architecturally through economic decay. Frome's economy successfully diversified after the decline of its woollen cloth industry into other industries, such as printing.

BATH, MILSOM STREET 1895 36457
Bath is perhaps the most remarkably architecturally unified town in England, a quite outstanding example of Georgian town planning. Who can forget the stunning architectural impact of the vast Royal Crescent or the sinuously curving Lansdown Crescent? From about 1720 to the 1820s an unique and mercifully complete Georgian city overlaid the medieval city. The city's origins go back well before the Roman conquest of Britain in the first century AD. It appears that the springs were sacred to the Celtic Goddess, Sul. It is not surprising as these hot springs on the site of the city issuing forth over a quarter of a million gallons each and every day must have appeared a marvel of nature. The ancients clearly took a view that is still held today that if the waters tasted awful (and they do) they must be curative!

dorset

From the deep valleys and woodlands of the west, to the high chalk downlands with their ancient ridge paths, to the lowland heaths of the east where rare birds and butterflies can be found in the heather and gorse, Dorset remains unspoiled and rural. The county is, however, bounded to the south by a long coastline of exquisite beauty and variety, from the fossil cliffs of Lyme Regis on the Devon border to the vast expanses of Poole Harbour to the east.

By Victoria's reign the Dorset coastal resorts were thriving. Nearly everything that goes to make up a traditional seaside holiday was in place: the sea bathing, lounging in deck chairs, promenades and piers, excursions to local beauty spots and boating trips.

DORCHESTER, HIGH STREET EAST 1891 28512
Dorchester, the capital of Dorset, has associations with the writers Thomas Hardy and William Barnes, and as if that was not enough,
it boasts a street pattern at its heart which was laid down by Roman settlers. Dorchester is one of the best examples of a Roman town, and hardly
a year passes without some pieces of its Roman archaeology coming to light.

DORCHESTER, CORNHILL 1891 28514

The County Town of Dorset has a splendid variety of architecture, ranging from medieval through Georgian to Victorian. A stroll around its streets and tree-lined walks can recapture the mood of Hardy's famous novel 'The Mayor of Casterbridge'. Dorchester, as the name suggests, was an important settlement during the heyday of the Roman Empire, and the surrounding countryside is rich in Roman remains. Just south of the town is the amphitheatre of Maumbury Rings, which was to Dorchester 'what the Coliseum was to Rome', according to Hardy.

WEYMOUTH, THE SANDS 1909 61597

Fashionable Georgian society flocked to this otherwise peaceful village in the wake of King George III, as did later Victorian gentlefolk. Weymouth, situated on a spit of land between the sea and Radipole Lake, is really a seaside town par excellence, for no street is more than a few minutes stroll from the water. By late Victorian times Weymouth had already acquired its reputation as a family resort and here they all are; the adults, formally-dressed even for the beach and promenade; nannies giving babies some fresh air, and older children - perhaps the most liberated of all from the constrictions of beach fashion - enjoying the waves as children still do now.

DORSET

LYME REGIS, THE COBB 1912
65040

This great sea wall and jetty dates back to the time of King Edward I, though stormy seas have meant its constant rebuilding and repair. Much of the present structure dates from 1825. It is famous for its association with the novel and film 'The French Lieutenant's Woman'. A guidebook from the 19th century advised visitors to Lyme to arrive by sea, for 'the journey by land is too tedious to be undertaken for pleasure'. The steamship from Weymouth would call at Lyme in the morning of its longer voyage to Torquay and Dartmouth, returning in the evening. The remarkable Miss Mary Anning brought fame to Lyme when she discovered an ichthyosaur near Charmouth in 1811. Fossil hunting remains a lucrative industry here to this day.

BOSCOMBE, THE PIER 1908 61191
Boscombe developed to the east of Bournemouth in mid-Victorian times, attracting the wealthy and fashionable, including Sir Percy Florence Shelley, the son of the poet. Mineral springs added to Boscombe's attraction for those seeking an improvement to health, though it never became the spa that it aspired to be.

BOURNEMOUTH, FROM THE PIER 1897
40559
Bournemouth, once in Hampshire but now in Dorset, did not exist two hundred years ago. In 1810 Lewis Tregonwell built a house on lonely heathland close to the mouth of the River Bourne. During the years that followed other wealthy Hampshire gentlemen followed his example. It was to be the very end of the century before the town became popular as a holiday resort.

POOLE, THE CUSTOM HOUSE 1904
52814

Poole developed alongside the finest natural harbour in England; it did not become a holiday resort for many years, but retained its importance as a port and merchant centre, having strong links with Newfoundland. In 1747 a valuable cargo of tea was seized by the revenue men and stored in the Custom House. A band of well-armed smugglers attacked the building, stealing the tea and putting the revenue men to flight.

SWANAGE, THE BEACH 1918 68090
The coming of the railway in 1885 brought tourists to Swanage in greater numbers. Described by Thomas Hardy as '...a seaside village lying snugly within two headlands as between a finger and a thumb', Swanage was also the centre of the Isle of Purbeck stone quarrying industry.

DORSET

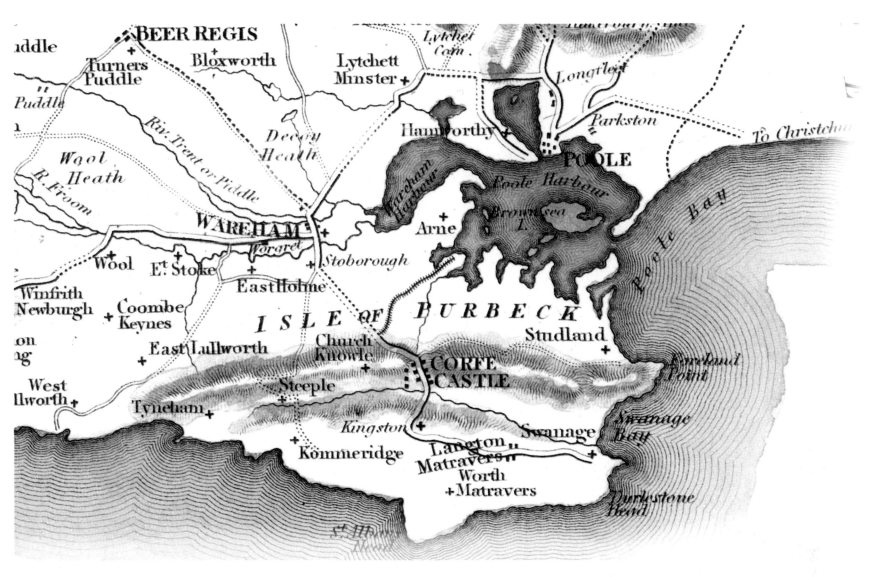

BOURNEMOUTH,
THE SWANAGE BOAT
1908   61183
A great number of coastal
steamers carried
passengers along the
Dorset coast, visiting the
resorts of Poole, Swanage,
Weymouth and Lyme
Regis, to name a few.

wiltshire

Wiltshire is not overburdened with large towns and cities, which is probably why it is such a pleasant county. From the commercial bustle of Swindon, historic Salisbury and scattered market towns to sleepy, thatched archetypal English villages such as Castle Combe, Wiltshire is a county of contrasts.

Being landlocked, the county had no sea-port to facilitate trade but Wiltshire is crossed by trade routes from major conurbations such as London, including the modern M4. Much of the county's early industry was centred around the weaving of broadcloth and other types of fabric, and wool was the catalyst for much of Wiltshire's wealth, which funded its grandiose buildings.

Other industries were brewing, motorcar manufacture and food production - the name 'Wiltshire Ham' carries connotations of flavour even today. In modern times the main centre of industry is Swindon, a town which has successfully reinvented itself since the closure of its famous Great Western Railway locomotive works. Tourists flock to Wiltshire to enjoy attractions such as Longleat, Bowood and other stately homes, the prehistoric monuments of Stonehenge and Avebury, and the medieval Salisbury Cathedral.

SWINDON, MEN LEAVING GWR 1913 S254607

Wiltshire's main centre of industry is Swindon. Until comparatively recent times, it was industry of the metal-bashing variety as the Great Western Railway had their locomotive works here. Some of England's most famous steam engines first turned their wheels leaving this factory. As railway services contracted, a major rationalisation in the 1980s saw the unthinkable happen and the Swindon works closed. But the town has triumphed over adversity, and Swindon is now a commercial centre with computer, finance and motorcar industries offering plenty of employment.

SALISBURY, POULTRY CROSS AND SILVER STREET 1906 56359

The only city in Wiltshire is Salisbury. This beautiful place, sitting alongside the banks of the river Avon, has inspired poets and painters over the centuries. The cathedral itself is simply awesome. Yet the city of Salisbury did not exist before the cathedral was built. Two miles north is a low hill, standing alongside the Avon. This was originally an Iron Age fort, built around 500 BC, that was discovered by the Romans when they arrived. Appreciating its ideal defensive position they built Sorviodunum at the meeting of north/south and east/west roads. This became Old Sarum. Later the Normans built a cathedral and a royal castle. However there were constant problems, particularly with water supplies. When Bishop Herbert Poore decided to build a new cathedral a less exposed position was perceived to be a good idea. A spot close to a good water supply was considered vital, thus the present site was chosen and the former cathedral at Old Sarum abandoned and dismantled.

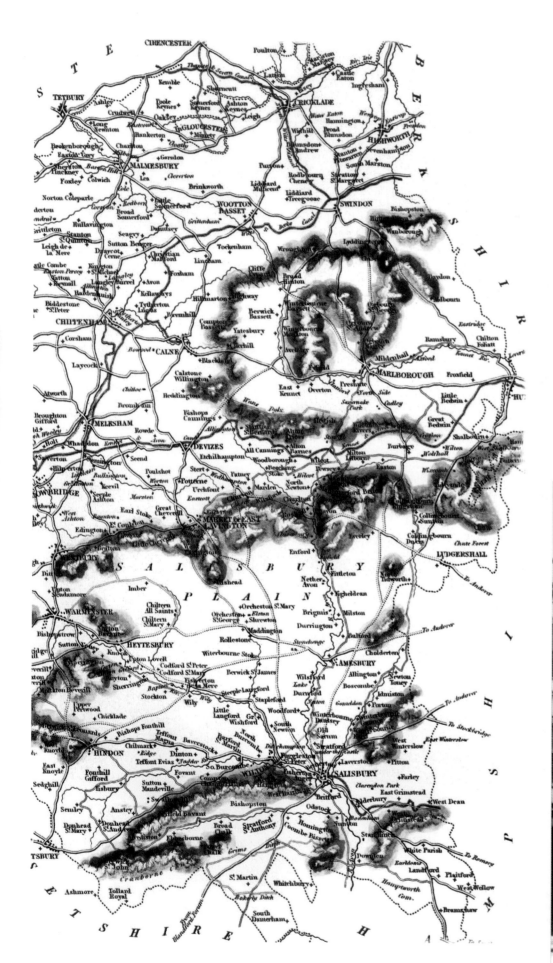

WILTSHIRE

SWINDON, FLEET STREET 1913
S254608

Swindon has a population well in excess of 200,000. The town has had three distinct development phases. Before the arrival of railways Swindon was an agricultural community. Then the Great Western Railway arrived. The establishment of its main locomotive works there, at the junction of several railways, caused a huge explosion in the population. New Town was built, including a model village of some three hundred houses for the GWR employees. These homes were built with stone excavated from Box Tunnel and are now designated a Conservation Area. Then contraction of the railway network brought savage cuts and ultimately closure of the works in the 1980s. But Swindon is nothing if it is not resilient. Today the electronics industry is a large employer, and again the town is growing fast. Being close to the motorway network makes it an ideal place for distribution companies; almost any company seems to find some benefit from locating in Swindon.

TROWBRIDGE, FORE STREET AND TOWN HALL 1900 45342

Weaving was a trade that made Trowbridge wealthy, but it was not without its troubles, as was noted in St James' churchyard. Here there is a monument to Thomas Helliker who, at nineteen years old, was executed in 1809 as the leader of riots over the introduction of power looms.

SALISBURY, FISHERTON STREET 1906 56360

When the noted diarist Samuel Pepys visited Salisbury in 1668, '...guided all over the plain by the sight of the steeple,' he noted that 'the river runs through every street.' This was a system of small canals that provided for water and drainage.

hampshire

Few counties in the south of England offer such diversity of scenery and character as Hampshire. Much of it remains unspoilt, and even today it still seems to embody the heart and soul of the English countryside. Stretching from the genteel yachting haven of Lymington in the west to Surrey's manicured commuter belt in the east, it has often been said that Hampshire has something for everyone. With its charming villages, rolling farmland, scenic forests and gentle river valleys, Hampshire's attractions are certainly many and varied. And, of course, there is the county's bracing coastline, scattered with monuments to the past and a permanent reminder of how this country has defended itself against attack over the centuries.

BASINGSTOKE, CHURCH STREET 1904 52129

Basingstoke's role as an important market centre dates back to medieval times; it was established as a borough in 1622 when James I
granted the town a charter giving it a weekly market and a twice-yearly fair. By the late 17th century it was a prosperous market town.
Despite its somewhat drab image, Basingstoke has some interesting and distinctive buildings - particularly in Winchester Street and London Street.
As a town, Basingstoke has been growing since the early part of the 20th century, in the last 40 years or so it has become the fastest growing town
in western Europe, its population increasing from 17,000 in the early 1950s to 67,000 in 1981.

ANDOVER, HIGH STREET 1908 60092 Medieval Andover was established around a market which stands nowadays in the shadow of the 19th-century church of St Mary, built in the Early English style by a former headmaster of Winchester College, and described as the best Victorian church in Hampshire.

ROMSEY, OLD CORN EXCHANGE 1932 85040
To the right of Romsey's Corn Exchange, built in 1864, is a glimpse of Romsey Abbey, which until the mid 16th century was home to a Benedictine order of nuns. At the time of the Dissolution the abbey was saved from destruction by the people of Romsey, who paid £100 for it. The abbey was founded in AD907 by Edward the Elder, son of Alfred the Great, but the main part of the building was built in the 12th century by Henry de Blois, Bishop of Winchester.

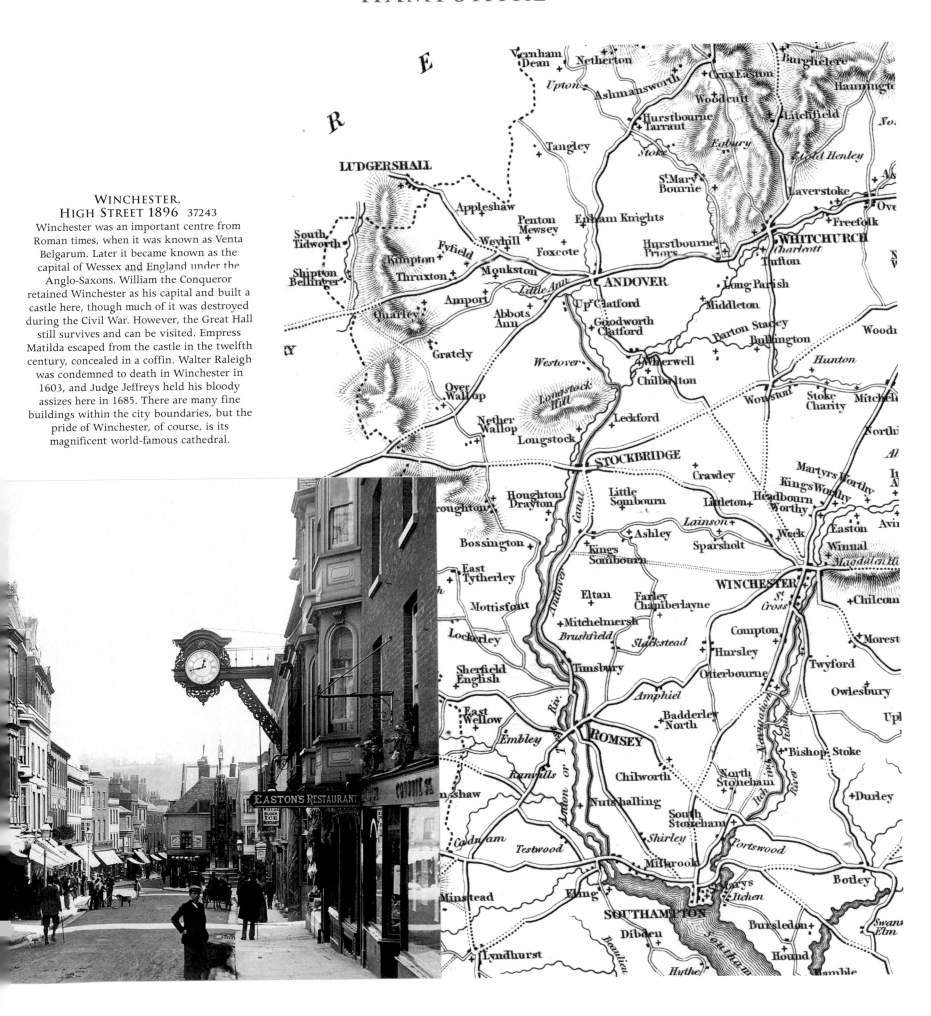

WINCHESTER, HIGH STREET 1896 37243

Winchester was an important centre from Roman times, when it was known as Venta Belgarum. Later it became known as the capital of Wessex and England under the Anglo-Saxons. William the Conqueror retained Winchester as his capital and built a castle here, though much of it was destroyed during the Civil War. However, the Great Hall still survives and can be visited. Empress Matilda escaped from the castle in the twelfth century, concealed in a coffin. Walter Raleigh was condemned to death in Winchester in 1603, and Judge Jeffreys held his bloody assizes here in 1685. There are many fine buildings within the city boundaries, but the pride of Winchester, of course, is its magnificent world-famous cathedral.

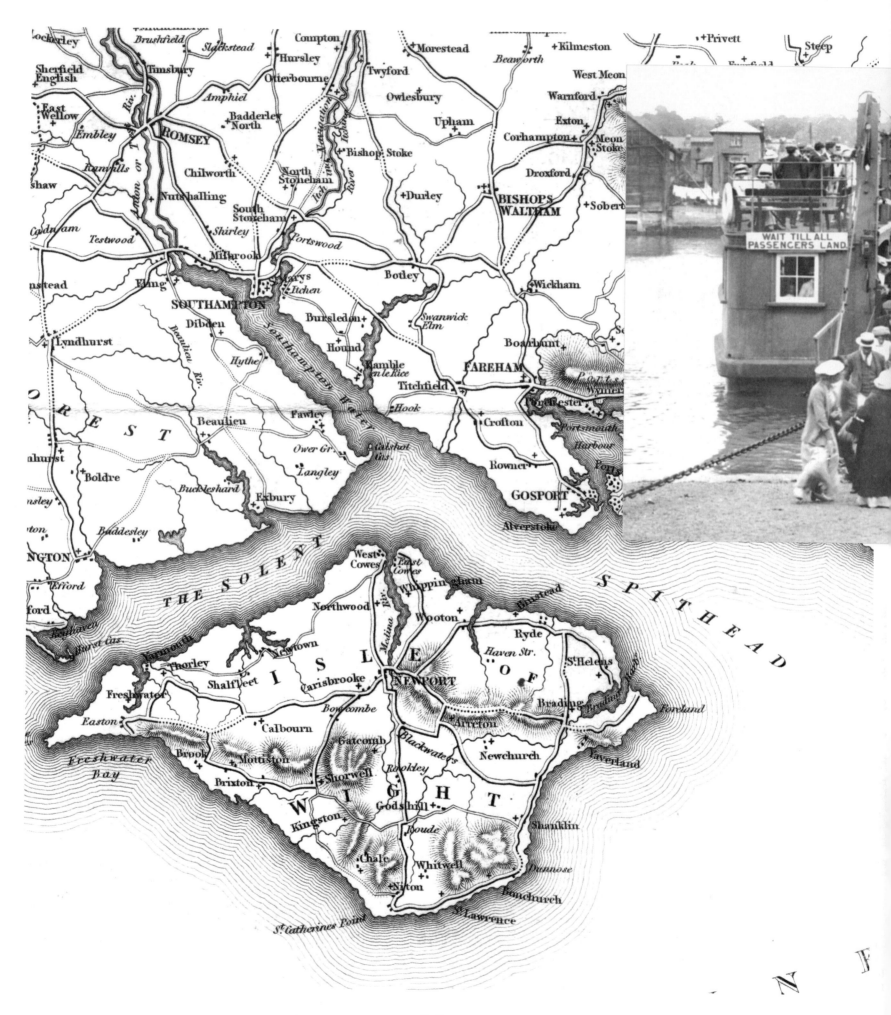

COWES, THE FERRY 1913 66313

Many visitors gain their first impression of the Isle of Wight as they land by ferry from Southampton. Cowes harbour is a fine natural anchorage which has been appreciated by sailors for centuries. The early local historian Sir John Oglander remarked that he saw some 300 ships riding at anchor there in 1620. The two Cowes, situated on the west and east banks of the River Medina, are famous throughout the world as a centre for yachting. The town's yacht club became the Royal Yacht Club in 1820 on the accession of George IV, a notable member, and in 1933 the club became the prestigious Royal Yacht Squadron. The yachting regatta first took place off Cowes in 1776. Some attempt was made in Georgian times to turn Cowes into a fashionable watering place but it never happened, because of the limited suitability of the sea bathing available. Bathing is possible along some of the beaches at Cowes, particularly at Gurnard Bay, but the currents are strong and the shoreline shelves steeply. Cowes' reputation as a yachting paradise overwhelmed all real attempts to open up the town as a simple holiday resort, but in the 19th century the close proximity of Queen Victoria's holiday retreat of Osborne House made the town most fashionable, and a large number of hotels were built to cater for the increased number of tourists.

SOUTHAMPTON, ROYAL PIER PAVILION 1908 60415

Acting as a symbolic gateway to the world, Southampton is situated on the wide estuary of two great rivers - the Test and the Itchen. In the golden days of ocean-going travel, this internationally famous waterway provided first-time visitors to the shores with one of their first glimpses of English soil. Today the waterfront is more heavily industrialised, and the great passenger liners are certainly fewer. But the sense of maritime history is still tangible as one recalls the names of the great liners that once plied these historic waters - the 'Mauretania', the 'Aquitania', the 'Queen Mary' and the 'Queen Elizabeth' amongst them. The ill-fated 'Titanic' sailed from Southampton in 1912, and the 'Great Eastern' was moored in Southampton Water before her maiden voyage in 1861.

LYNDHURST, HIGH STREET 1908 60106

In the Victorian era Lyndhurst was a quiet town. The 'capital' of the New Forest, it is now a bustling tourist base at the heart of this wooded region. Soaring above the buildings of the town is the spire of St Michael and All Angels' Church, designed by William White, who worked under George Gilbert Scott. Inside the church is a fresco by Lord Leighton, said to be the first in an English church since the Reformation. Alice Liddell, the original inspiration for Lewis Carroll's Alice in Wonderland, is buried here.

NEWPORT, HOLYROOD STREET 1913 66322

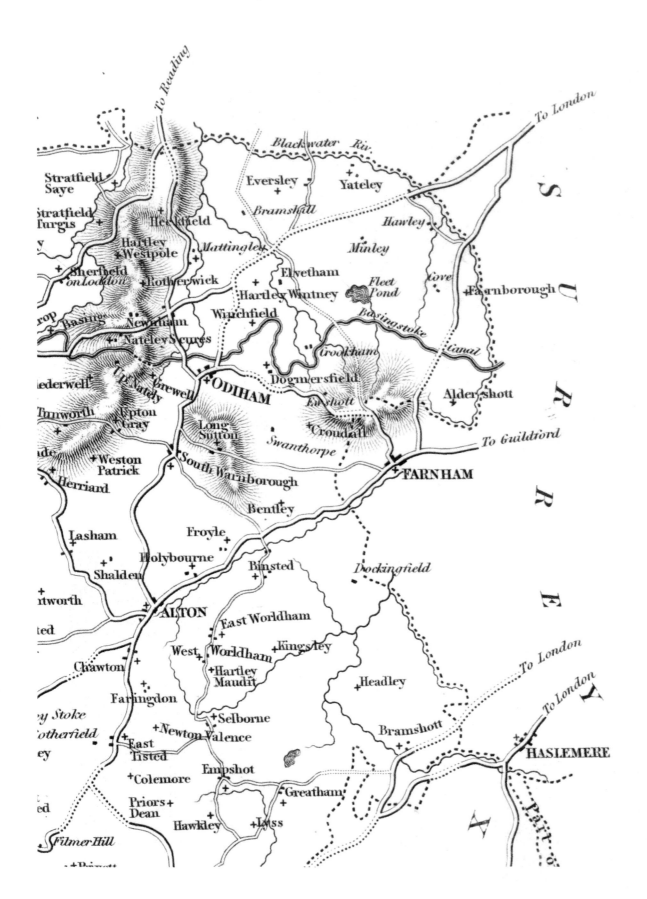

FARNBOROUGH, LYNCHFORD ROAD 1919 68913
In the early 19th century, Farnborough was a small village in the north-east of Hampshire that had changed little over the centuries since the Domesday survey of 1086. In 1811 the population was 360, and by 1851 it was still only 477. It was a small farming community with some potteries nearby, such as at Cove. Farnborough stood in the midst of a vast heath; the main Reading to Guildford road ran through it, and a turnpike road from London to Winchester ran close by.

ALDERSHOT, UNION STREET 1918 68360

The town of Aldershot is largely Victorian. In those early days some of the streets had shops on one side and barracks on the other. The older part of the town lies close to the railway station. Before assuming the role of the first military town in Britain, Aldershot was no more than a pretty village comprising a church, a manor house and several farms. Nearby was an area of open heathland.

ODIHAM, CEMETERY HILL 1910 63011

French soldiers were held as prisoners of war at Odiham during the Napoleonic Wars, living in a camp dug out of an old chalk pit. The churchyard contains the graves of several prisoners. Many of Odiham's houses are a mixture of Georgian and Tudor; some are timber-framed, which was common before local bricks came into use in the 18th century.

Sussex

The character of Sussex has changed considerably over the past two centuries. From being one of the least known of the southern counties, it has become possibly the most popular. During the late 18th century, the small towns, agricultural villages and hamlets adjoining the coast began to develop into fashionable Georgian watering places as the fashion for holidays beside the sea gained popularity. Initially, because of the limited number of visitors, only a few places could benefit from the emergence of seaside tourism. Brighton was the first Sussex resort town to develop, but the fashion for sea bathing soon spread to affect adjacent areas of the Sussex coastline. While development at Hastings was slow, and the spectacular investment at Bognor by the entrepreneur Henry Hotham was a financial disaster, Worthing and Eastbourne developed into fashionable Georgian towns. By the beginning of the Victorian period, resort development was becoming a significant element in the overall economy of Sussex. The opening of the London to Brighton Railway in 1841 rapidly changed Brighton from a fashionable watering place into a centre of mass entertainment. As an antidote to Brighton's lively entertainment, the more select watering place became a particular phenomenon of the Sussex coastline. Both Worthing and Eastbourne continued to actively encourage middle-class Victorian visitors. Today the urban conurbation that stretches along the Sussex coastline is one of the most developed areas in Britain.

WINCHELSEA, WESLEY TREE 1912 64938
Winchelsea is located on a sandstone rock, similar to the site of Rye, and was occupied in 1289 after Old Winchelsea was finally overwhelmed by the sea. New Winchelsea was laid out in a grid system, but only the north-eastern quarter is currently used. Several buildings of the 17th and 18th centuries were recorded in 1937, some of which had medieval vaults beneath them.

EASTBOURNE, FROM THE PIER 1906 56684

Before becoming a seaside resort under the patronage of the Cavendishes (the Dukes of Devonshire) after about 1850, the village of East Bourn, well inland, had its focus around the parish church of St Mary. William Cavendish, from 1858 Duke of Devonshire, had successfully lobbied to get a railway line into Eastbourne, and the first station opened in 1849. He had the appropriately named Terminus Road laid out to link the station with the sea front.

**BOGNOR REGIS,
THE PARADE AND PIER
1911** 63793
The first seaside resort development at Bognor was at Hothampton, well away from the fishing village; here in 1787 Sir Richard Hotham laid out terraces and his house in a park, Hotham Park. His resort linked with the sea via Waterloo Square, originally modestly named Hotham Fields. Development stagnated after his death in 1799, however, and subsequent growth was piecemeal.

CHICHESTER, MARKET CROSS 1892 29983
Little of the Roman town or medieval city remains, as Chichester was almost entirely rebuilt by the end of the 18th century. The ancient county town is connected to the sea by the Chichester Canal. Chichester was a walled Roman town, Noviomagus, and its main streets still follow its Roman layout. The streets meet at the medieval Market Cross, a gift to the town from the Bishop of Chichester, Edward Storey, in 1501.

LITTLEHAMPTON, THE BEACH 1898 42574
Littlehampton's role as a port at the mouth of the River Arun goes back to the 11th century; it prospered then in importing Caen limestone from Normandy for church and castle building. It continued as a thriving, if small, coastal port, and still does so, besides catering for large numbers of pleasure craft and yachts.

ARUNDEL, THE CASTLE AND BRIDGE 1902
48790A

Markets and ports were an important part of the trading network during the Middle Ages. Indeed, by Domesday Arundel was already an important river port. Its impressive castle, rebuilt in the 19th century, overlooks the Arun valley. With its fine chalk cliffs at Amberley, this is possibly the most scenic of all the river valleys in Sussex.

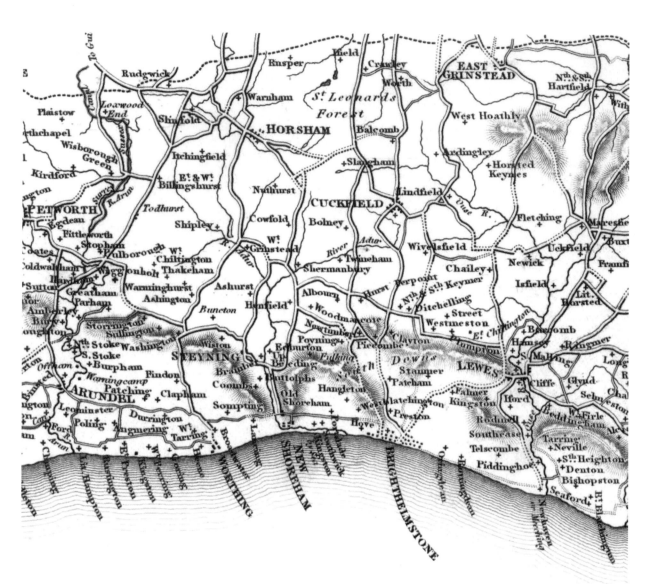

WORTHING, THE BANDSTAND AND PARADE 1899 44882

Seaside piers were unique to Britain. They initially consisted of a jetty leading to a landing stage for boats, but they soon became fashionable promenades extending over the sea.

By the 1860s, their popularity, combined with technical innovation derived from the railways, led to the construction of purpose-built pleasure piers. Worthing pier, opened in 1862, was the first of these new-style piers in Sussex. By the end of the Victorian period band concerts were a popular form of entertainment at most resorts. This resulted in the erection of a wide variety of ornate iron bandstands, many of which were selected from illustrations in pattern books issued by the various ironworks. W Macfarlane of Glasgow erected the iron 'birdcage' bandstand on the Esplanade at Worthing in 1897.

BRIGHTON, THE BEACH 1898 41890
Once a fishing village known as Brighthelmstone, the Sussex seaside metropolis of Brighton became popular as a sea-bathing resort after Dr Richard Russell moved there in 1754 to supervise his sea-water cures. The town boomed under the patronage of the Prince Regent, who in 1785 leased Brighton House, a farmhouse north of the Old Steyne or the fishing port. The farmhouse was enlarged by Henry Holland, and from 1813 John Nash turned it into the romantic Hindu/Mahometan domed and minaretted fantasy palace we see today.

HORSHAM, WEST STREET 1898 42851
Horsham was described as a borough in the early 13th century, and it had become one of the chief towns in the county by the 17th and 18th centuries. In 1844 Ann Holland was sold by her husband for 30 shillings in Horsham Market Square; the purchaser, a Mr Johnson, sold his watch to meet the price.

CRAWLEY, THE FAIR 1905 53325
Crawley was originally a village which grew in importance during the coaching era; its fair was held twice-yearly. It was designated a 'New Town' in 1947. Today it is in easy reach of London, and also of Gatwick Airport.

A JOURNEY AROUND ENGLAND

UCKFIELD, HIGH STREET 1902 48198
Uckfield was a centre of the iron industry in the 17th and 18th centuries, and was well-known for its brickworks into the twentieth century.

HAILSHAM, HIGH STREET 1890 44955
Hailsham grew markedly after the railway arrived, and was noted for its rope factories, breweries and cattle market, which at one time was one of the largest and busiest in the county.

EASTBOURNE, THE PIER 1901
48065
Like any self-respecting seaside resort, Eastbourne acquired a pier; piers were originally used solely as landing stages for sea trips and boats, but soon became sources of entertainment in their own right. Eastbourne's was designed by Eugenius Birch in 1866.

EAST GRINSTEAD,
LONDON ROAD 1914 66750
East Grinstead, a Wealden market town founded during the early 13th-century woodland clearances, was recorded as a borough by 1235.

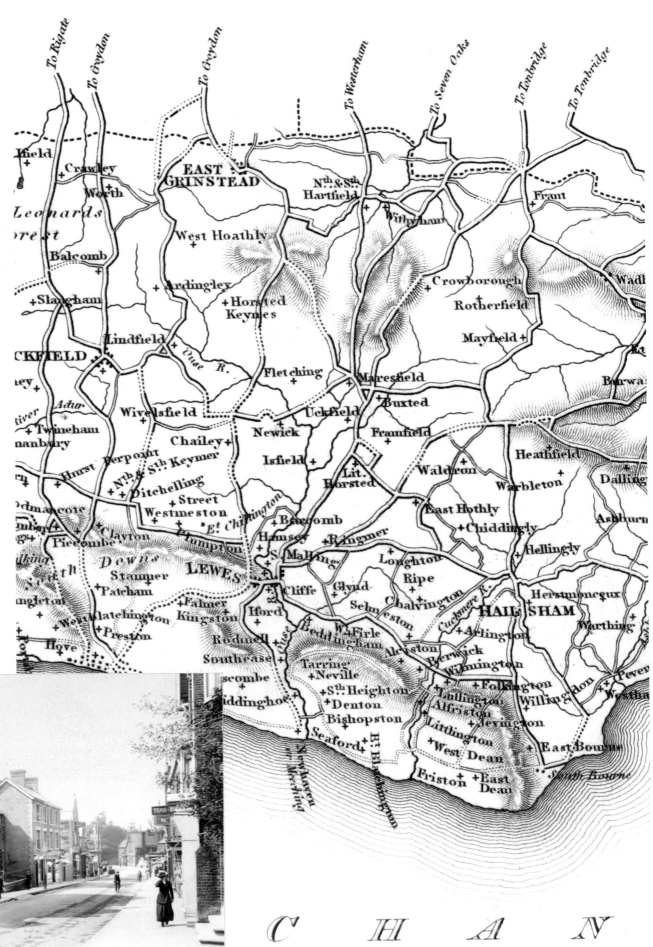

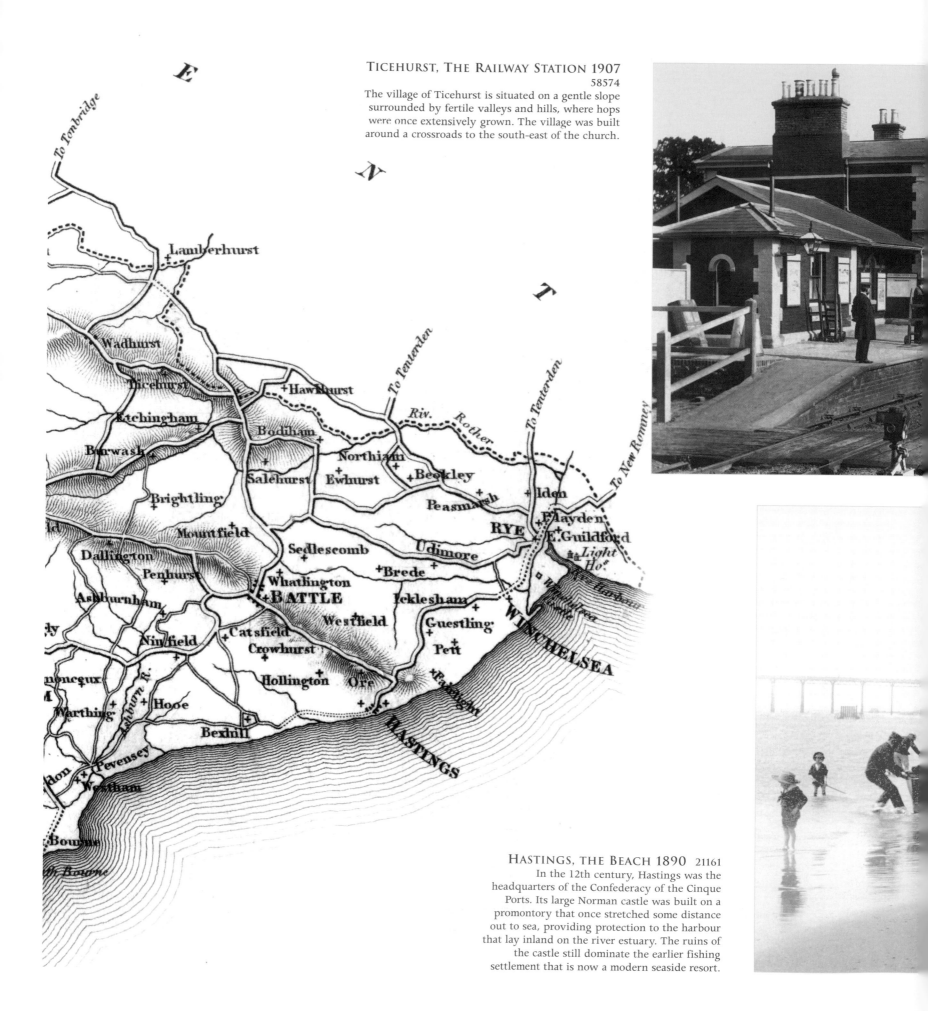

TICEHURST, THE RAILWAY STATION 1907
58574
The village of Ticehurst is situated on a gentle slope surrounded by fertile valleys and hills, where hops were once extensively grown. The village was built around a crossroads to the south-east of the church.

HASTINGS, THE BEACH 1890 21161
In the 12th century, Hastings was the headquarters of the Confederacy of the Cinque Ports. Its large Norman castle was built on a promontory that once stretched some distance out to sea, providing protection to the harbour that lay inland on the river estuary. The ruins of the castle still dominate the earlier fishing settlement that is now a modern seaside resort.

BATTLE, HIGH STREET 1921 71507
William I founded Battle Abbey on Senlac Moor, the site of the Battle of Hastings.
The small town of Battle grew up when the people who built and maintained
the abbey and the buildings settled there.

Surrey

'This county of Surrey presents to the eye of the traveller a greater contrast than any other country of England. It has some of the very best and some of the worst lands, not only in England, but in the world'. So wrote William Cobbett in his 'Rural Rides', in 1822, when Surrey was primarily an agricultural county. His reference to the 'worst lands' referred to the unproductive heaths in the north-west of Surrey which were to be largely exploited by the military later in the century, for depots and training purposes.

Cobbett could not have foreseen the transformation that would occur within a few years of his death. In 1838 the first steam-hauled train carrying fare-paying passengers trundled into Woking Common station, heralding the start of a new era which relentlessly brought London into Surrey. By the middle of the 19th century the expansion of the railway network across the county enabled passengers to reach the capital in just over an hour from the southern extremities of the county. The commuter age was born, and increasingly new suburbs were built along the route of the rail lines.

The advent of motor transport also caused Surrey's countryside to be irrevocably changed by building development and road programmes, with new roads, including the M25, M3 and M23 cutting through the landscape. Ironically it was a Surrey man, Henry Knight of Farnham, who was credited with building the first British car in 1895.

GOMSHALL, THE MILL 1904 51810

GUILDFORD, HIGH STREET 1895 35060A
Guildford's High Street lies along the important prehistoric routeway that runs
along the chalk hills from Hampshire to Canterbury.
This route was used by chert and flint traders of Neolithic times,
and has continued in use through the passing ages.

WALTON-ON-THAMES, THE SWAN HOTEL 1908
60037
In the 19th century 'messing about on the river' was one of the most popular recreations, and the River Thames was crowded with punts and rowing boats. Ladies were especially keen on punting and the fame of the 'English Punt Girl' spread far and white. Apparently pink and white were the preferred colours to wear.

BAGSHOT, VILLAGE CHILDREN 1903 50991
Bagshot had a reputation as a haunt of highwaymen, who preyed on travellers on the Portsmouth Road.

CHERTSEY, THE SCHOOL 1908 60940
The Thames-side of Chertsey was once famous for its abbey, now almost entirely vanished; its stone was used for the building of Hampton Court.

GUILDFORD, MARKET STREET 1904 51858
Most of Market Street was taken up by the now demolished Red Lion. The hotel was mentioned by that seasoned traveller John Aubrey in the early 17th century, and was a frequent stopping place for Samuel Pepys.

FARNHAM, SOUTH STREET 1904 51602A
During the 18th century hops were of prime importance to Farnham, which had five breweries and more inns than any other town in Surrey.

GOMSHALL, THE MILL 1904 51810
'Gomeselle' was mentioned in Domesday, at which time a mill already existed at the site. Gomshall Tanneries were known world-wide, but were taken over and closed in 1988.

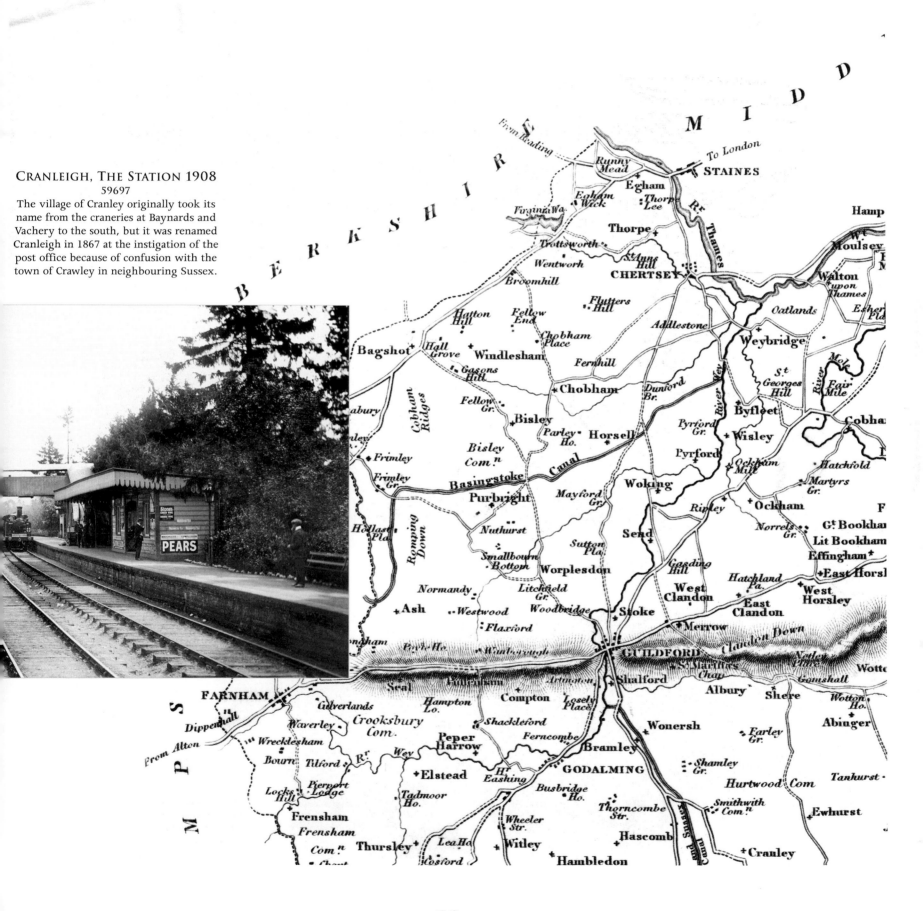

CRANLEIGH, THE STATION 1908
59697
The village of Cranley originally took its name from the craneries at Baynards and Vachery to the south, but it was renamed Cranleigh in 1867 at the instigation of the post office because of confusion with the town of Crawley in neighbouring Sussex.

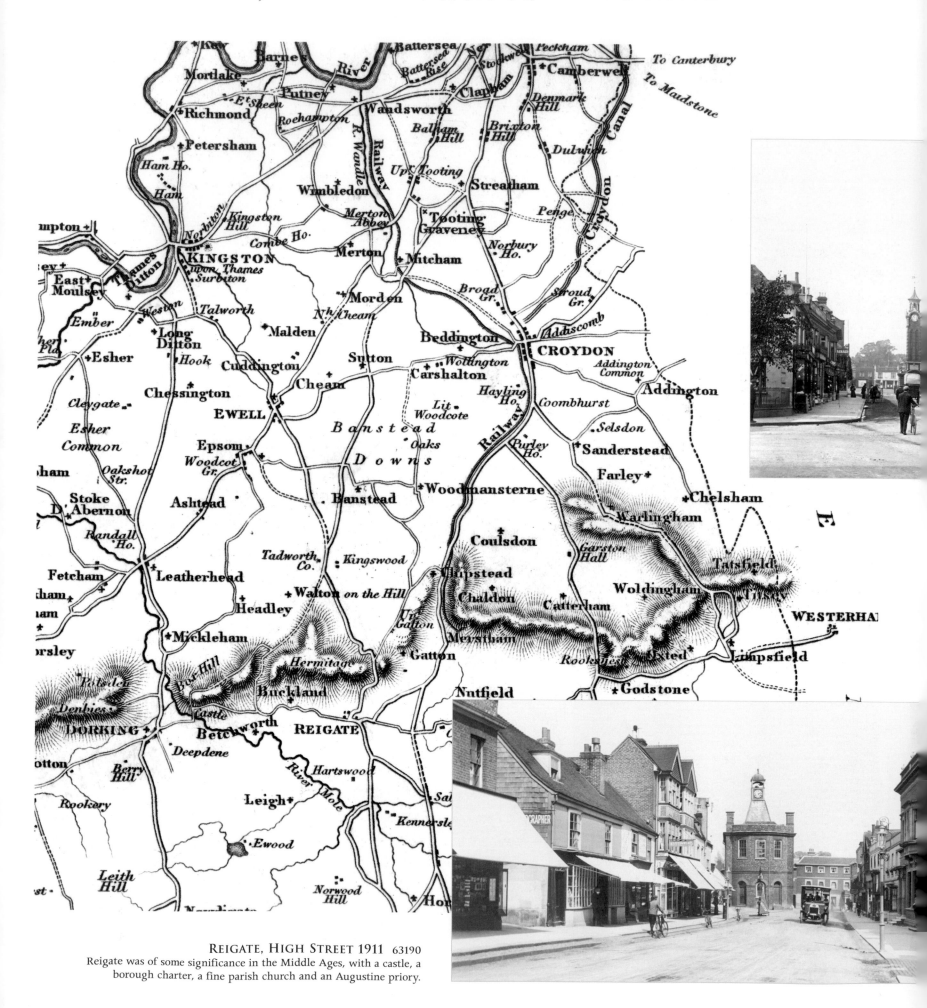

REIGATE, HIGH STREET 1911 63190
Reigate was of some significance in the Middle Ages, with a castle, a
borough charter, a fine parish church and an Augustine priory.

KINGSTON UPON THAMES, MARKET PLACE 1906 54705
Kingston upon Thames preserves its medieval market place and the pattern of narrow streets around it reminds us that it was an Anglo-Saxon royal town where seven kings of Wessex were crowned.

EPSOM, HIGH STREET 1907 58595
Famous for its racecourse, home of the Derby, Epsom was also a fashionable spa in the 18th century thanks to the restorative powers of Epsom salts, found in the water of a local spring.

DORKING, HIGH STREET 1905 53334
Dorking's architectural heritage has been decimated since the Second World War although the 15th-century White Horse coaching inn still stands in the High Street.

LEATHERHEAD, NORTH STREET 1906 54878
Leatherhead gets its name from two Saxon words meaning 'public ford', referring to its importance in ancient times as a crossing place near the River Mole.

kent

Kent ranks ninth in size among the counties of England, and perhaps no county has more history within its boundaries than Kent. Separated from Europe by only 21 miles of sea, it has been invaded by foreign powers over the centuries. It has also been the target of several failed invasions from the time of the Napoleonic Wars in the 19th century to 1940, when Hitler's invasion plans envisaged landing on the Kent coast.

Until the early 19th century, settlement in Kent was mainly rural, in small communities. In 1821 only one-fifth of the county's population lived in one of the main 12 towns. Thus the past has bequeathed a rural landscape of independent farmsteads, hamlets and rural villages. Although much agricultural land in Kent is under the plough nowadays, there are still areas of orchards and also of hop gardens and their associated oast houses, so typical of the country landscape of the past. Hops were first introduced by Flemish weavers in the 16th century. In the days when beer was a staple drink for the working classes, there was a great demand for hops from the brewers.

Kent has over 126 miles of coastline, with the great advantages of good communications to the large centres of population around London and generally warm, dry summers. The development of the railways in the mid 19th century changed the county; the lines stretched out from London to the nearest stretches of coastline, and in 1851 four of the ten largest seaside resorts in Britain were located in Kent - Margate, Ramsgate, Dover and Gravesend. Broadstairs, Folkestone, Herne Bay and Deal grew in the next few decades.

HEVER, CHIPPENS BANK ROAD 1906 53556
Today Hever is best known for its moated castle, restored at the beginning of the 20th century by Lord Astor, who also created a Tudor-style village nearby. Hever Castle was owned by the family of Anne Boleyn, the second wife of Henry VIII. Henry confiscated it after Anne's execution and later gave it to his fourth wife, Anne of Cleves, after divorcing her.

CANTERBURY, THE WEST GATE 1921 70330
Canterbury Cathedral has been an object of pilgrimage for many centuries.
The object of the journey was the shrine of St Thomas à Beckett,
famously martyred in 1170 by four of Henry II's over-zealous knights.

GRAVESEND, KING STREET 1902 49028

Gravesend was once a busy riverside town giving easy access to London. It was at its peak before steam traffic grew in the 1850s. In 1820 the ferry across to Tilbury and up river to wharves in London's East End carried over a million passengers a year, and 44 horse-buses would meet the ferries running regularly to the Medway towns and Maidstone.

MAIDSTONE, ALL SAINTS CHURCH 1862 1481

Maidstone owes its importance to its strategic position where the road from London to the coast crosses the River Medway - the bridge across the river is in the centre of the town. An ancient settlement, it was granted its first charter in 1548, and since the early 19th century has been the county town of Kent - most departments of the County Council are here. The early narrow streets of the medieval layout have since been widened to cope with modern traffic. The congestion has now been partly relieved by the motorways by passing the town.

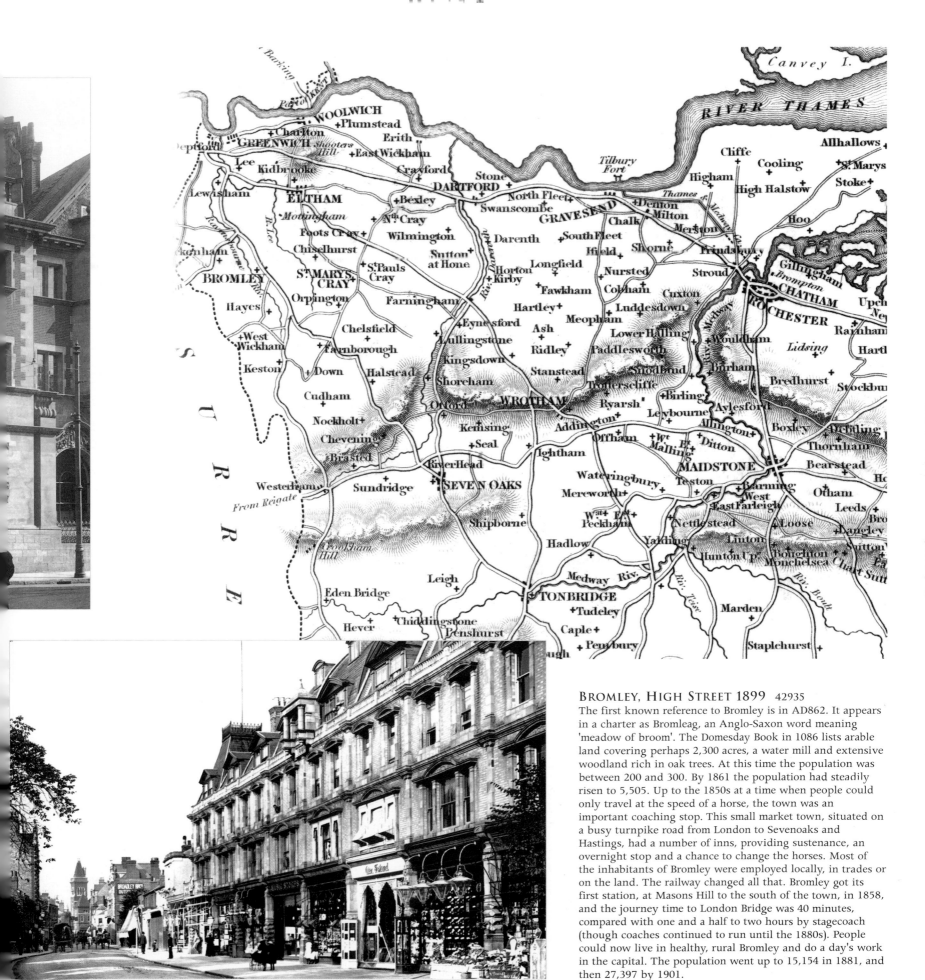

BROMLEY, HIGH STREET 1899 42935

The first known reference to Bromley is in AD862. It appears in a charter as Bromleag, an Anglo-Saxon word meaning 'meadow of broom'. The Domesday Book in 1086 lists arable land covering perhaps 2,300 acres, a water mill and extensive woodland rich in oak trees. At this time the population was between 200 and 300. By 1861 the population had steadily risen to 5,505. Up to the 1850s at a time when people could only travel at the speed of a horse, the town was an important coaching stop. This small market town, situated on a busy turnpike road from London to Sevenoaks and Hastings, had a number of inns, providing sustenance, an overnight stop and a chance to change the horses. Most of the inhabitants of Bromley were employed locally, in trades or on the land. The railway changed all that. Bromley got its first station, at Masons Hill to the south of the town, in 1858, and the journey time to London Bridge was 40 minutes, compared with one and a half to two hours by stagecoach (though coaches continued to run until the 1880s). People could now live in healthy, rural Bromley and do a day's work in the capital. The population went up to 15,154 in 1881, and then 27,397 by 1901.

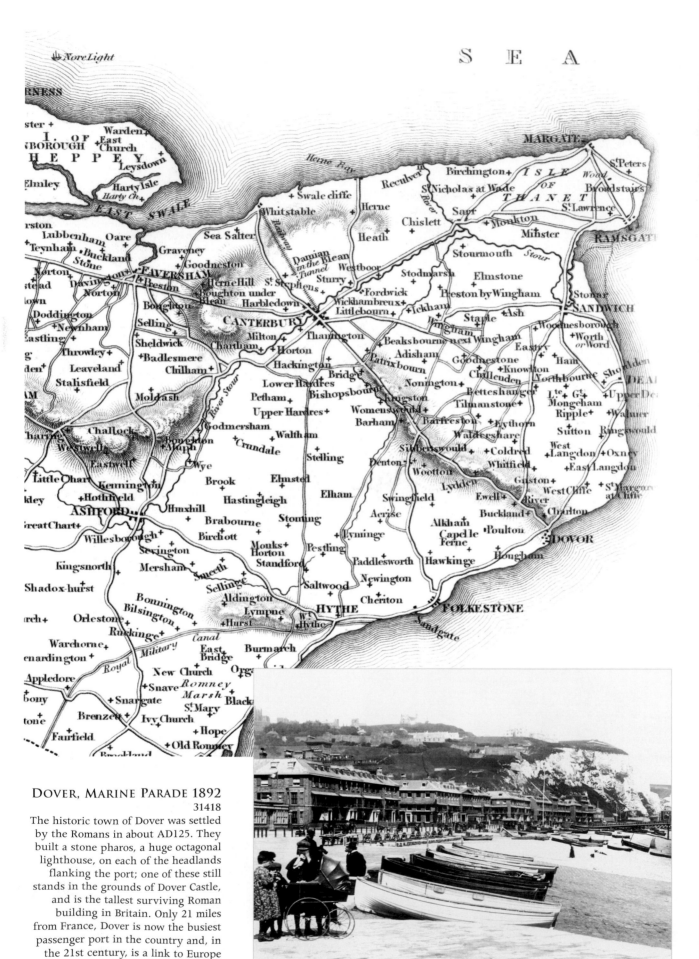

MARGATE, THE SANDS 1906 54758

The earliest Kent seaside resort was Margate, popular in the 1730s through its easy direct access by boat from London. Thanks to cheap rail and paddle-steamer fares in the 19th century, it became a magnet for Cockney day-trippers. The original Margate fishing villages expanded, and large hotels were built around the jetty and harbour area, as seaside holidays became popular.

DOVER, MARINE PARADE 1892
31418

The historic town of Dover was settled by the Romans in about AD125. They built a stone pharos, a huge octagonal lighthouse, on each of the headlands flanking the port; one of these still stands in the grounds of Dover Castle, and is the tallest surviving Roman building in Britain. Only 21 miles from France, Dover is now the busiest passenger port in the country and, in the 21st century, is a link to Europe via the Channel Tunnel.

RAMSGATE 1907 58272

Ramsgate was once a small fishing harbour, but it came into prominence with the building of the great stone harbour in 1749 as a refuge for shipping from the dangers of the Goodwin Sands. In Tudor times Ramsgate had developed links with Ostend and the Baltic, and in the 19th century it became a 'Royal Harbour'.

FOLKESTONE, THE LEAS 1901 48052

Folkestone, originally a small fishing village, developed as a resort when the S E Railway arrived from London in 1843, which also helped the harbour develop as a cross-channel port to Boulogne. The town was generally regarded as a rather superior, exclusive resort for middle-class visitors. This scene illustrates the costume and decorum of the period. As a bathing resort, Folkestone had a shingle beach at sea level, whilst on the cliff top behind was the Leas promenade and extensive lawns. The cliff railway provided a welcome link for the less energetic visitor.

middlesex

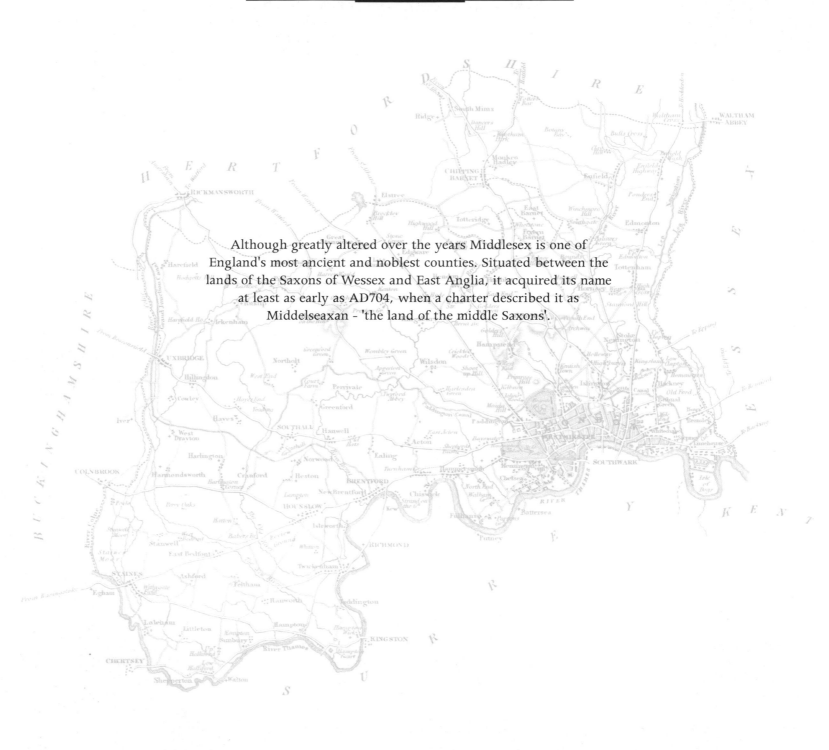

Although greatly altered over the years Middlesex is one of
England's most ancient and noblest counties. Situated between the
lands of the Saxons of Wessex and East Anglia, it acquired its name
at least as early as AD704, when a charter described it as
Middelseaxan - 'the land of the middle Saxons'.

MIDDLESEX

HAMPTON, THE BRIDGE 1890 27212

Many consider that the south-western corner of the county, alongside the Thames, is Middlesex at its loveliest. The Thames has always been important as a boating centre; for centuries it was used as a great water highway, along which many of the greatest figures of English history were transported. Regular yachting regattas are held at Hampton, and many owners keep their boats nearby. Hampton lies about four hours of cruising time from the centre of London. Hampton boasts a long history of famous residents. Sir Christopher Wren lived and worked here, designing St Paul's and recreating London after the Great Fire of 1666.

SUNBURY, THE MAGPIE HOTEL 1890 23560

Sunbury is a Thameside village, shared between Middlesex and Surrey; it expanded considerably during the last century. Kempton Park, now a venue for horse-racing, was once a royal residence. It became a fashionable place to reside during the 17th century, and there are a number of fine houses in the town.

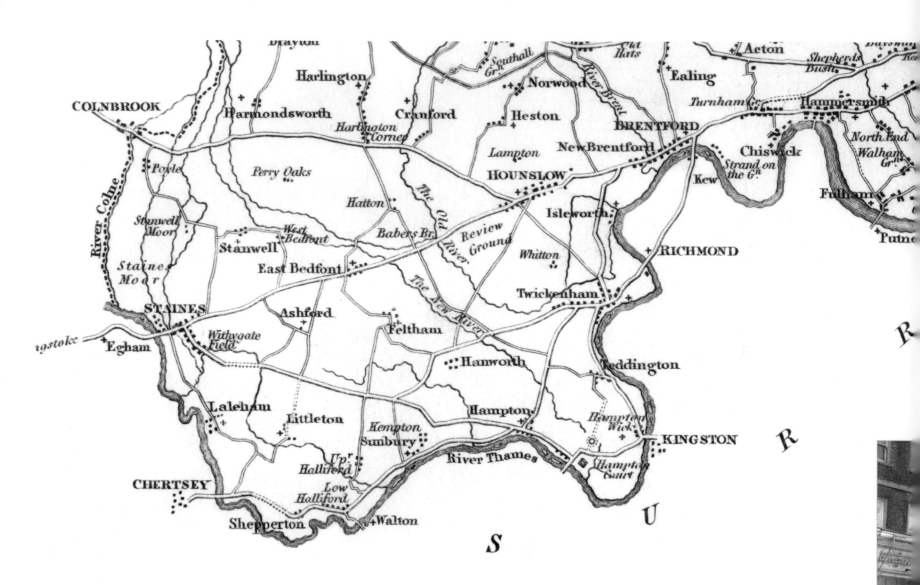

TWICKENHAM, THE ISLAND
1890 23535

In the last two hundred years this once-modest village has grown into a considerable town, lining miles of the river with streets and villas. A number of writers have found Twickenham an inspiring place in which to work. Charles Dickens wrote parts of 'Oliver Twist' at Ailsa Park Villas, and Dickens' literary hero Henry Fielding wrote 'Tom Jones' - one of the earliest of English novels - in a long-vanished house in Back Lane. It was in a Twickenham drawing room that George IV, when Prince of Wales, secretly married his mistress Maria Fitzherbert. This action was contrary to the Royal Marriages Act, for George was under 25 and Maria was a Roman Catholic. Although they lived as a couple afterwards, neither Parliament nor the Royal Family recognised their union. George subsequently married Caroline of Brunswick, though on their separation he lived once again with Maria. Maria Fitzherbert, an uncrowned Queen of England, died at Brighton in 1837.

MIDDLESEX

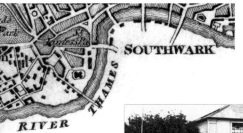

TEDDINGTON, THE BRIDGE 1899
43050

The Thames is tidal as far as Teddington; many Londoners are fond of the sight of the water tumbling over the famous weir. Nearby is the biggest lock on the river. It is still a busy water passage, with a great many pleasure craft passing through each day. Just over a hundred years ago, the Thames and its network of canals were used as much for transporting goods as for pleasure boating. Teddington's population grew from around 1,000 inhabitants in mid-Victorian times to over 25,000 just a century later. Many found it a pleasant town to live in, not too far from London. One famous resident was R D Blackmore, the author of 'Lorna Doone' and 'Christowell', who worked here as a market gardener, writing his novels in his spare time.

STAINES, HIGH STREET 1907 57997

Historically, Staines marked the end of the jurisdiction of the City of London over the river. Staines was very much an agricultural area towards the end of Queen Victoria's reign. Staines, like so many Middlesex towns, stands on one of the principal coaching routes out of London - the Exeter Road. Most of the old coaching inns, of which there were many, have now disappeared, ended by the construction of the railway. Sir Walter Raleigh was found guilty of treason in the old Market House at Staines, which has since been demolished. A plague had prevented the Court from holding the trial in London.

buckinghamshire

Buckinghamshire is a county that falls easily into two parts, with the chalk Chiltern Hills defining the north edge of the southern part. As soon as you drop northwards off the Chiltern scarp you are in the Midlands, where the open field farming of the Middle Ages dominates all the way from Wendover to the Northampton border. The landscape to the south is completely dominated by the Chilterns, a range of chalk hills that march across the south of the county. Amid this landscape are some fine market towns; being so close to London, commuter railway lines arrived in the later 19th century and led to very considerable growth, only contained by the adoption of the Metropolitan Green Belt in 1959.

**CHESHAM, HIGH STREET
1921** 70538
Chesham nestles at the head of the River Chess in a deep cut valley, and has been a market town since 1257, when the High Street and Market Place were laid out. The branch of the Metropolitan Railway with its terminus at Chesham opened in 1889.

AYLESBURY, MARKET SQUARE 1921 70552

Aylesbury effectively took over from a declining Buckingham as the county town in Henry VIII's reign, when the summer assize courts transferred here to the geographical centre of the county. This ancient hill town prospered in the 18th century and much of the historic core has survived. The heart of the old town is around St Mary's Church, built on the site of an Anglo-Saxon minster. The livestock market continued in the Market Square until 1927.

AYLESBURY, THE AYLESBURY ARM OF THE GRAND UNION CANAL 1921
70564

The Grand Junction Canal, now the Grand Union, was built between 1793 and 1805 to link Birmingham with the River Thames and London. Numerous branch canals were constructed to it, including the Aylesbury branch which finally opened in 1815. An immediate consequence was the halving of coal prices in Aylesbury!

WENDOVER, COLDHARBOUR COTTAGES, TRING ROAD 1899 44771

Wendover, a small market town, grew up where a valley route emerges from the Chiltern Hills. Great things were expected for the town when the Wendover Arm of the Grand Junction Canal opened in 1797, but it leaked and was a failure. The Metropolitan Railway arrived in 1892, and the town at last expanded.

BUCKINGHAM, MARKET SQUARE 1949 B280004
Much of Buckingham was destroyed by a disastrous fire in 1725; remote at the north-west corner of the county, it declined and lost its county town status to Aylesbury. The Town Hall, rebuilt in 1783, is crowned by a gilded swan.

CHESHAM, HIGH STREET 1903 49238
Chesham grew up at the junction of streams that feed the
River Chess. Noted for its watercress beds, the town also had a
number of watermills. Other industries included lace-making,
paper-making, straw-plaiting and wood-ware, such as malt shovels.

**HIGH WYCOMBE,
FROGMORE SQUARE
1921** 70607
Situated in the narrow
valley of the River Wye,
this medieval borough
developed into a major
corn market. The arrival of
the furniture industry,
based on the 18th-century
planting of the Chiltern
beech woods, led to
considerable Victorian
expansion from the
Georgian core of the town.

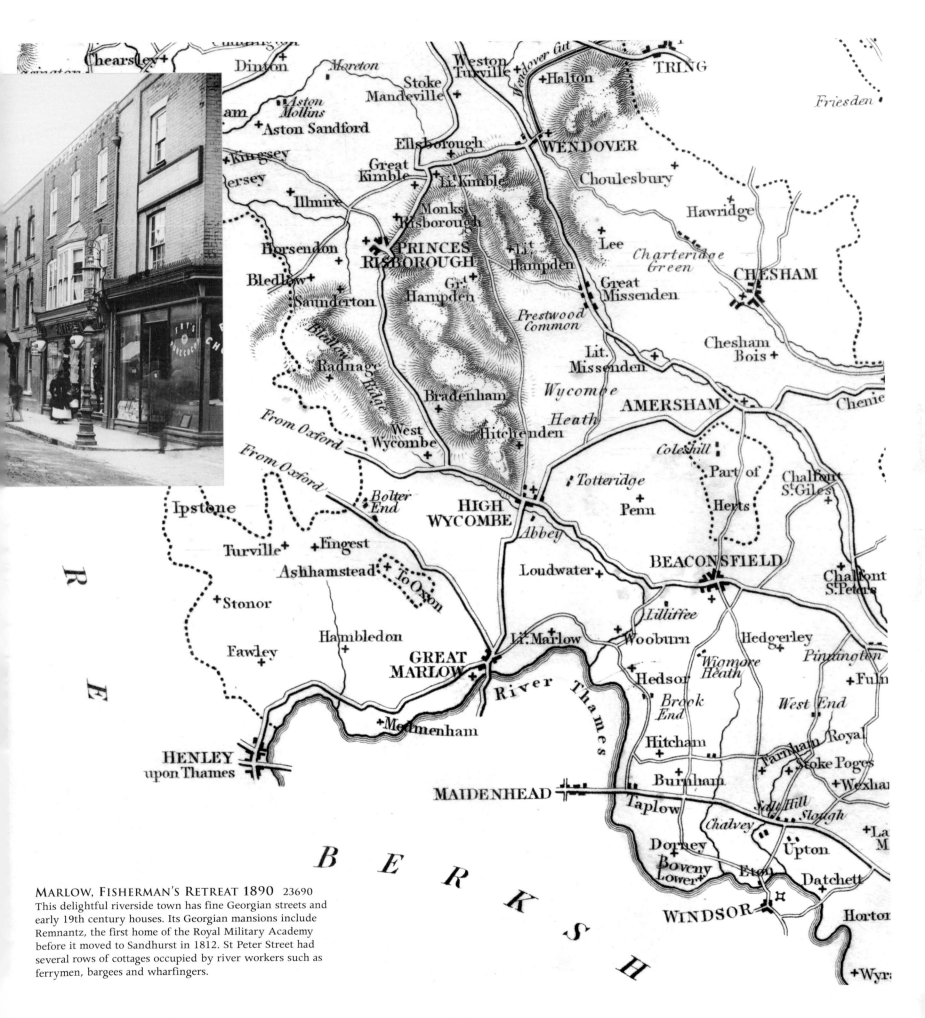

MARLOW, FISHERMAN'S RETREAT 1890 23690
This delightful riverside town has fine Georgian streets and
early 19th century houses. Its Georgian mansions include
Remnantz, the first home of the Royal Military Academy
before it moved to Sandhurst in 1812. St Peter Street had
several rows of cottages occupied by river workers such as
ferrymen, bargees and wharfingers.

berkshire

Small though it is, Berkshire is packed with history. Burial mounds and Iron Age hill-forts are scattered over the landscape, and Britain's oldest road, the Ridgeway, traces a line across open downland country above the Thames. Later, William the Conqueror built Windsor Castle, one of the county's most prominent landmarks.

Between the Middle Ages and the 17th century Berkshire witnessed great activity in the wool and cloth trade. Newbury's historic church of St Nicholas was built by John Winchcombe, described as 'the richest clother England ever had'. Berkshire also played its part in the agricultural revolution of the 18th and 19th centuries. Jethro Tull, who invented the seed drill and the horse-drawn hoe, worked on his inventions at Prosperous Farm, just outside Hungerford.

For the next 150 years or so the map of Berkshire gradually changed as canals, roads and railway lines threaded their way across the county. What we now know as the A4 was established as the Bath Road, its rough, rutted surface significantly improved by the introduction of turnpike trusts. Coaching inns began to appear along the route and towns and villages in the vicinity of the road grew in size and importance. Running parallel to the Bath Road through Berkshire were two other lines of communication: Brunel's Great Western Railway marched cross country towards Bristol, and the Kennet and Avon Canal, completed in 1810 at a cost of one million pounds, cut through the heart of west Berkshire. In the 19th and 20th centuries Berkshire witnessed even greater changes as traffic gradually became heavier, new roads and motorways began to spring up everywhere, and the population of the county increased dramatically as thousands of new homes were built within its boundaries.

READING, CAVERSHAM LOCK 1912 64648
Reading is famous for the Huntley and Palmer biscuit works, once one of the town's biggest employers. For many years the Thames played an important part in the success of the firm, carrying biscuits downstream to London docks.

READING, MARKET PLACE c1870 R13001
Reading's Market Place survives more or less intact today. Overlooking it is the magnificent 15th-century tower of St Lawrence's Church, founded in 1121.

HUNGERFORD, HIGH STREET 1903 49385
Famous now for its many antique shops which line the broad High Street, Hungerford was given a fishing charter and a brass drinking horn by John of Gaunt, the Duke of Lancaster, who granted fishing rights to the town. The Kennet, running through Hungerford, was once described as 'a fayre river which yieldeth store of fishes and especiallie of troutes'.

HUNGERFORD, HIGH STREET 1903 49384
Two hundred and thirty-five years before this photograph was taken, Samuel Pepys visited the town and ate 'very good troutes, eels and crayfish' at the Bear Hotel. In 1688 William of Orange accepted the throne of England here.

ASCOT, THE GRANDSTAND 1901 46866
The village of Ascot has grown and developed in the
shadow of the racecourse. King Edward VII did much to
promote the race meeting at Ascot as a significant social
event; members of the Royal Family still drive through
Windsor Great Park to attend.

MAIDENHEAD, BOULTERS LOCK 1906
54083
This photograph captures the Edwardian gaiety of the Thames at Boulters Lock, a particularly fashionable spot; dozens of smart cruisers, punts and small craft parade before an admiring audience.

WINDSOR, RIVERSIDE GARDENS 1906 53721
Overlooked by Windsor Castle's famous Round Tower, Windsor Bridge was erected in 1822. Until the 20th century there was a toll - the living paid 2d, while the departed could be carried across by coffin for 6/8d!

oxfordshire

Lying at the heart of England, Oxfordshire boasts a rich heritage and a surprisingly varied mix of scenery. Its landscape encompasses open chalk downlands and magnificent beechwoods, picturesque rivers and canals bustling with activity, ancient towns of mellow stone and attractive villages set in peaceful farmland. In the south-west the country meets neighbouring Berkshire high on the downs, offering far-reaching vistas and fascinating links with the distant past. To the south-east lie the Chilterns, with their steep slopes and wooded hills. The countryside in the north-west of Oxfordshire seems isolated by comparison, with its wide views, rolling hills and dry-stone walls, while historic Banbury acts as a gateway to the Midland counties.

In earliest times the Ridgeway crossed the wild, windswept downland, possibly Britain's oldest road and now a popular long-distance trail. At the beginning of the 20th century Oxfordshire had a good network of roads and railways, and the Oxford Canal. The canal, built in 1790, linked Oxford with the Midlands. Brunel's Great Western Railway arrived in 1841, and Didcot became a major railway centre. A branch line was built to Oxford in 1844, which had been extended to the Midlands by 1852; other links served Thame, Woodstock and Witney. There was also a line between Banbury and Cheltenham. This network provided a faster and more efficient transfer of wood, stone, coal and agricultural produce to and from the Midlands and other parts of the country. Another major communications link through Oxfordshire is of course the River Thames, which has been used as a highway from earliest times.

OXFORD, CARFAX TOWER 1922 71997
A policeman directs traffic in the centre of Oxford. This is where four streets converge. Carfax is the Latin 'quadrifurcus' meaning 'four-forked'. Carfax Tower is where Charles II was proclaimed King in 1669.

OXFORD, CORNMARKET STREET 1922 71996

At the very heart of the county of Oxfordshire lies one of Britain's most beautiful cities. Originally known as Oxnaforda, the Anglo-Saxon Chronicle records that King Edward the Elder made Oxford a fortified frontier position defending Wessex from Danish attack. Oxford has attracted scholars since the end of the 12th century, and has grown and evolved as a place of learning and a treasure house of medieval architecture. During the Civil War Oxford was the Royalist stronghold as well as the seat of Charles I's parliament. In the 20th century Oxford witnessed sweeping changes. In 1912 William Morris built his first motorised vehicle in a workshop in Cowley; by the late 1930s the car industry had made an enormous impact on Oxford, with new housing estates built to accommodate the thousands of people who worked at the plant.

BANBURY, MARKET PLACE 1921 70572
The second largest town in Oxfordshire, Banbury has long been famous as the main meeting point of routes from the Midlands to London and Oxford. Banbury's spacious Market Place is overlooked by many buildings of different architectural styles.

OXFORD, CHRIST CHURCH 1922 72009
The college chapel of Christ Church is officially 'The Cathedral Church of Christ in Oxford', the smallest of all English cathedrals.

BICESTER, MARKET SQUARE c1955 B365001
Bicester still retains the feel of a county town. There is an interesting variety of architectural styles around the three-cornered Market Square. Sadly, several 18th-century fires destroyed many of the town's old timber buildings.

BURFORD, HIGH STREET c1955 B369011
Often described as the gateway to the Cotswolds, the picturesque town of Burford has changed little over the years. The High Street runs down between pollarded lime trees and mellow stone houses to the River Windrush. Charles II stayed here, possibly with Nell Gwynne, whose child was named the Earl of Burford.

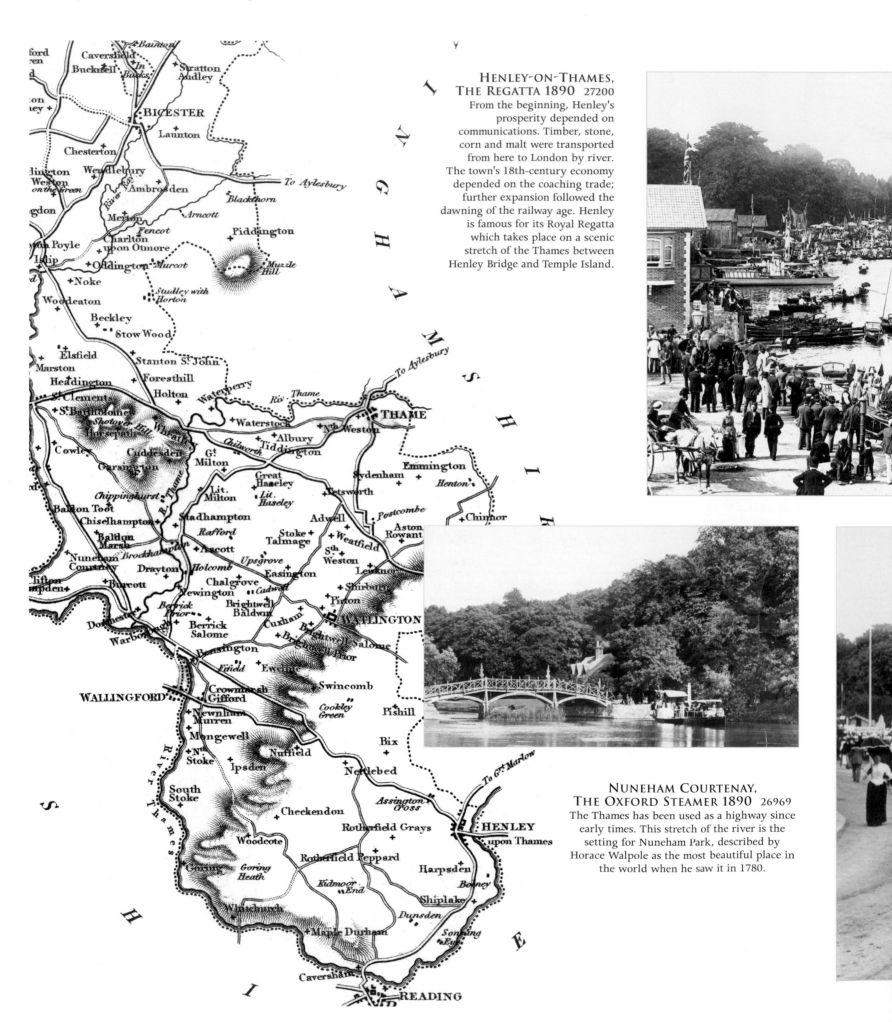

HENLEY-ON-THAMES, THE REGATTA 1890 27200

From the beginning, Henley's prosperity depended on communications. Timber, stone, corn and malt were transported from here to London by river. The town's 18th-century economy depended on the coaching trade; further expansion followed the dawning of the railway age. Henley is famous for its Royal Regatta which takes place on a scenic stretch of the Thames between Henley Bridge and Temple Island.

NUNEHAM COURTENAY, THE OXFORD STEAMER 1890 26969

The Thames has been used as a highway since early times. This stretch of the river is the setting for Nuneham Park, described by Horace Walpole as the most beautiful place in the world when he saw it in 1780.

OXFORDSHIRE

GORING, THE VILLAGE 1899 42991
This sprawling riverside village lies between the beech-clad hills of the Chilterns and the windswept slopes of the Berkshire Downs. The coming of the railway and Goring's close proximity to the river helped put the village on the map around the turn of the century.

HENLEY-ON-THAMES, REGATTA DAY 1899 43020
By the turn of the century Henley Regatta had become one of the major attractions of the English season. The course is 1 mile and 450 yards long, rowing upstream.

gloucestershire

The 15th-largest county in England, Gloucestershire's 800,000 acres offer some of the most varied and splendid scenery in Britain. Uplands such as Cleve Common spread beyond the Cotswold escarpment. Slimbridge - home to the Wildfowl Trust - and other wetlands are found along the Severn. Between the two is the flat vale that is one of the richest farm and market-gardening areas in the country, while further south steep stream-cut valleys radiate like spokes from Stroud and Nailsworth, towns that once generated industrial wealth. Tucked between the Severn and the Wye rivers, the Forest of Dean is a more mysterious area: a mixture of open land and twenty-four thousand tree-covered acres which became England's first National Forest Park in 1938, and which also has an industrial past where iron and coal were mined.

TEWKESBURY, CHURCH STREET 1907 59072
The 18th century Royal Hop Pole Hotel is featured in Charles Dicken's 'Pickwick Papers', when Pickwick and his three companions dine there on their way from Bristol to Birmingham.

94

GLOUCESTER, NORTHGATE STREET 1904 51988
Queen Elizabeth gave Gloucester the formal status of a port in 1580, but it was not until the completed construction of the Gloucester and Berkeley Canal
in 1827 that the city began to equal Bristol in importance as a grain port. The three commodious docks, the largest of which was opened in 1892,
remained busy until the eventual decline in trade in the 20th century.

BERKELEY, MARKET PLACE 1904 51750
The wide, straight street of Berkeley is lined with houses of the Georgian period or earlier, with the
19th-century Town Hall facing out onto the Market Place.

NEWENT, THE MARKET HOUSE c1950 N180012
At the centre of this bustling town is the late Tudor Market House, restored in the 19th century.
Supported on sixteen wooden pillars, its single, large, upstairs room is reached by a flight of outside stairs.

BRISTOL, THE CITY CENTRE 1900 45649C

This famous old city, situated seven miles up the Avon from the Bristol Channel, became the second most important city in England after London in medieval times. The navigable Rivers Avon and Severn gave the town its competitive edge. In 1552 Bristol's Merchant Venturers were incorporated, and from then on Bristol ships could, theoretically, be found anywhere in the world.

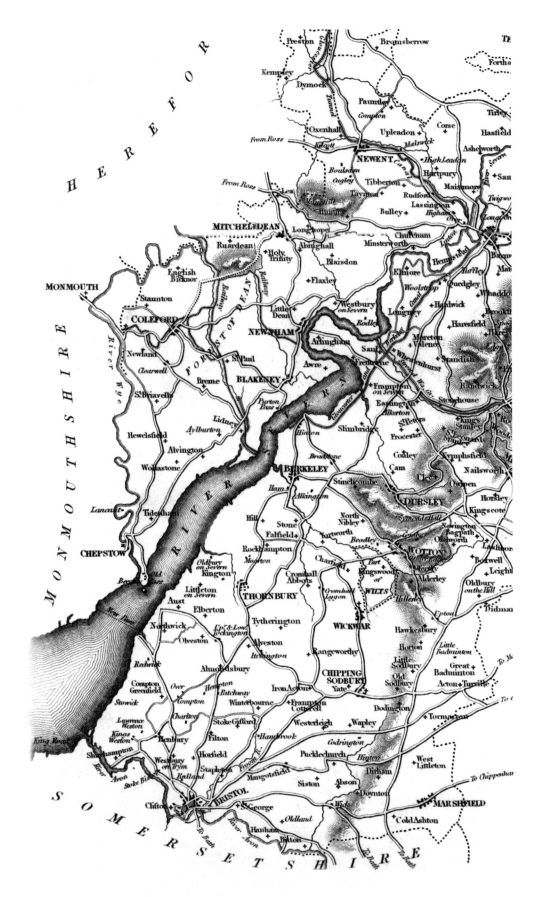

BRISTOL, PARK STREET 1900 45653

It was along Bristol's Park Street that the Philosophical and Literary Institution had its premises in the early years of the 19th century, and one of the first scientific lecturers was Humphrey Davy. Davy also belonged to the Bristol Library Society; its members included Samuel Taylor Coleridge, Robert Southey and William Wordsworth.

CHELTENHAM, HIGH STREET 1906 54319

Cheltenham was only a small market town until Captain Henry Skillicorn began to develop its potential as a spa from 1738. The town became fashionable after the visit of George III in 1788, and its reputation was made after the Duke of Wellington visited the spa in 1816, suffering from a liver disorder which was alleviated by 'taking the waters'. It is now famous for its Georgian architecture, annual festivals of music and literature, and the Cheltenham Gold Cup steeplechase.

CHELTENHAM, THE COLLEGE PLAYING FIELDS 1907 59038

Cheltenham's Cricket Festival takes place each August; the event dates back to 1877, when it was first held in honour of W G Grace.

GLOUCESTER, EASTGATE STREET 1931 83828

The remains of Roman Glevum lie beneath the city of Gloucester. An important port in medieval times, it was later overshadowed by Bristol. Gloucester Cathedral, however, remains one of the most beautiful buildings in Britain.

TEWKESBURY, CHURCH STREET 1907 59071

On the near side of the street is a motor vehicle whose registration numbers AB100 mark it as being one of the earliest to take to the roads in Britain.

WOTTON-UNDER-EDGE, LONG STREET 1903 49798
The right to hold a market and fair was granted to Maurice, Lord Berkely by Henry III, and this was responsible for the subsequent prosperity of the town.

CIRENCESTER, MARKET PLACE 1898 40965
Cirencester was known as Corineum in Roman times, when it was the second largest settlement in England. The parish church of St John the Baptist overlooks the town. Dating from the 12th century, its splendid tower was built in the early 15th century. Inadequate foundations meant that the tower began to show signs of instability even before it was completed and it had to be shored up with spur buttresses.

STROUD, HIGH STREET 1910 62676
Abundant, fast flowing streams made Stroud an important mill town in the Middle Ages, when water wheels turned the stones that ground the corn. By the 16th century the town was closely connected with the cloth trade, and became famous for the scarlet woollen fabric from which the uniforms of British soldiers were made.

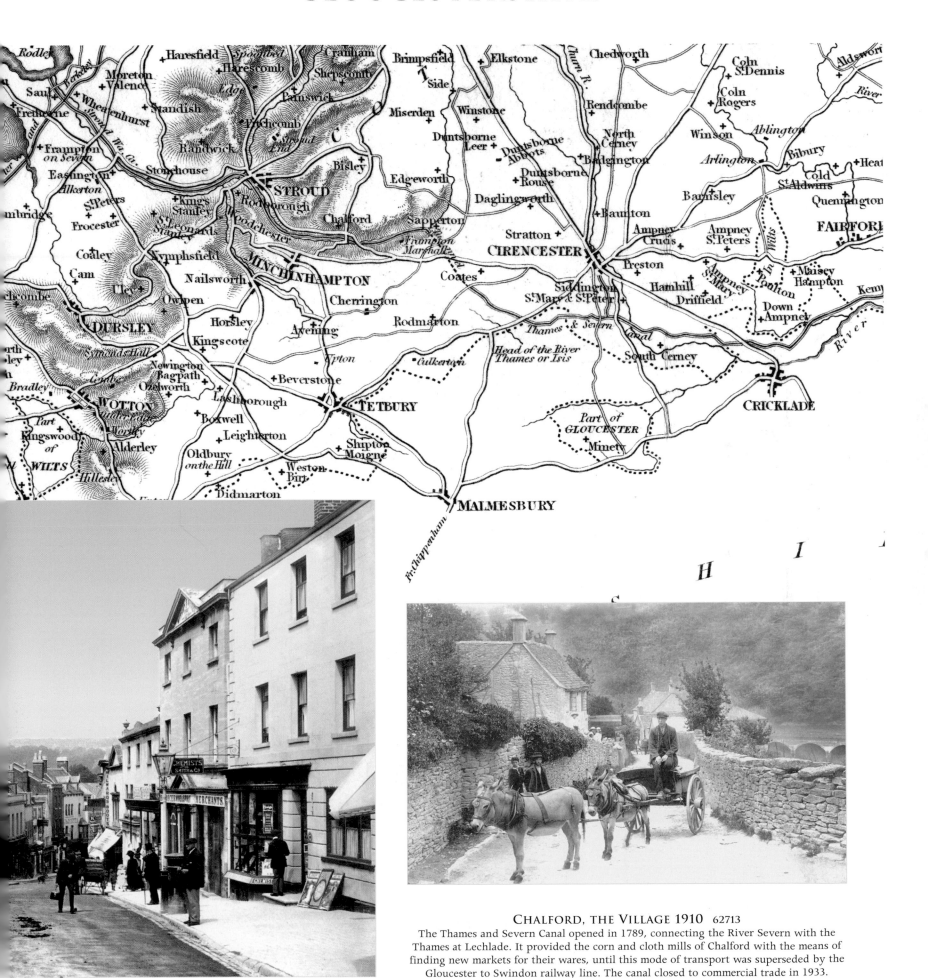

CHALFORD, THE VILLAGE 1910 62713
The Thames and Severn Canal opened in 1789, connecting the River Severn with the
Thames at Lechlade. It provided the corn and cloth mills of Chalford with the means of
finding new markets for their wares, until this mode of transport was superseded by the
Gloucester to Swindon railway line. The canal closed to commercial trade in 1933.

herefordshire

'Of all the counties England can record,
Few are so blessed as this of Hereford
For wheat and wool, and wood and water famed,
And for good cider very much esteemed.
Few counties can afford a better place
For fishing, fowling or the healthy chase:
England has not more rich or fertile fields,
None that a better annual produce yields...'

Lines written by Thomas Parker, a joiner living in Kington in the north-west of the county, around 1785.

LEOMINSTER, HIGH STREET 1904 51920
Leominster's church is magnificent, dating from the 12th century, and has some wonderful carvings. It also houses a ducking stool, which was last used in 1809 for a scolding wife called Jenny Piper - but it was not only used for nagging women. One pub sign in the town depicts a man (a cheating trader perhaps?) undergoing a ducking.

HEREFORD, HIGH TOWN 1891 29285
Nell Gwynne, orange seller, actress and mistress to Charles II, is believed to have been born in Hereford. Other places make the same claim, but the diarist Samuel Pepys mentioned a conversation with Nell in his diary in which she spoke of her early life in Hereford. He described her as 'pretty, witty Nell'.

HEREFORD, HIGH TOWN 1898 41751
High Town is still the main shopping area in Hereford. It was once known as the Butchery, where meat was sold.

LITTLE HEREFORD, THE CHURCH 1898 41745
Little Hereford was so called because the manor once belonged to the church at
Hereford. It sits beside the River Teme, and the church of St Mary Magadalene,
which was built in the 13th century, has been regularly flooded over the centuries.

BROMYARD, FROM THE STATION 1906 54301
Herefordshire has long been an important hop-producing region. In 1807
there were 660 acres of hop fields in the parish of Bromyard. A line of the
Worcester and Bromyard Railway Company was opened in 1877, and in 1900
there were 5 passenger trains a day serving this small community. The line
eventually closed in 1964.

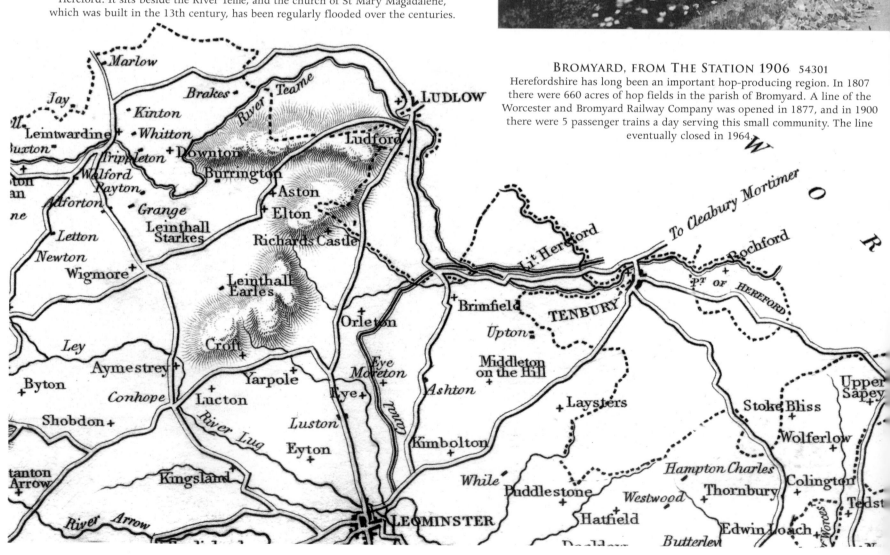

LEOMINSTER, DRAPERS LANE 1904 51922
In times past the cloth trade was an important local industry. A local woollen cloth was of such quality that it was known as 'Lemster Ore', and Queen Elizabeth I had her stockings woven from it.

Stourport

W E S T

orcester

ne
ere

ABBEY DORE, THE CHURCH 1898
41759
Today's church is only the remaining chancel and transept of an earlier building, originally a Cistercian abbey.

ROSS-ON-WYE, THE RIVER WYE 1901
47887
There is a story that Ross was once called Rose-town because it 'rose gradually up the hill from the river'. In fact it comes from the Welsh 'rhos' meaning hill or promontory.

HEREFORD, COMMERCIAL STREET
1891 29288
The name Hereford means 'the ford for the army'. Which army it was that gave the place its name we can only guess at. The cathedral was founded in AD 676; nearly 150 years later it became an important site of pilgrimage with the establishment of a shrine to St Ethelbert, who was murdered (probably by King Offa) in AD794. The cathedral houses the largest chained library in the world, with some 1,500 books and manuscripts dating back to the 8th century. The best known manuscript is the Mappa Mundi, one of the four oldest maps in the world.

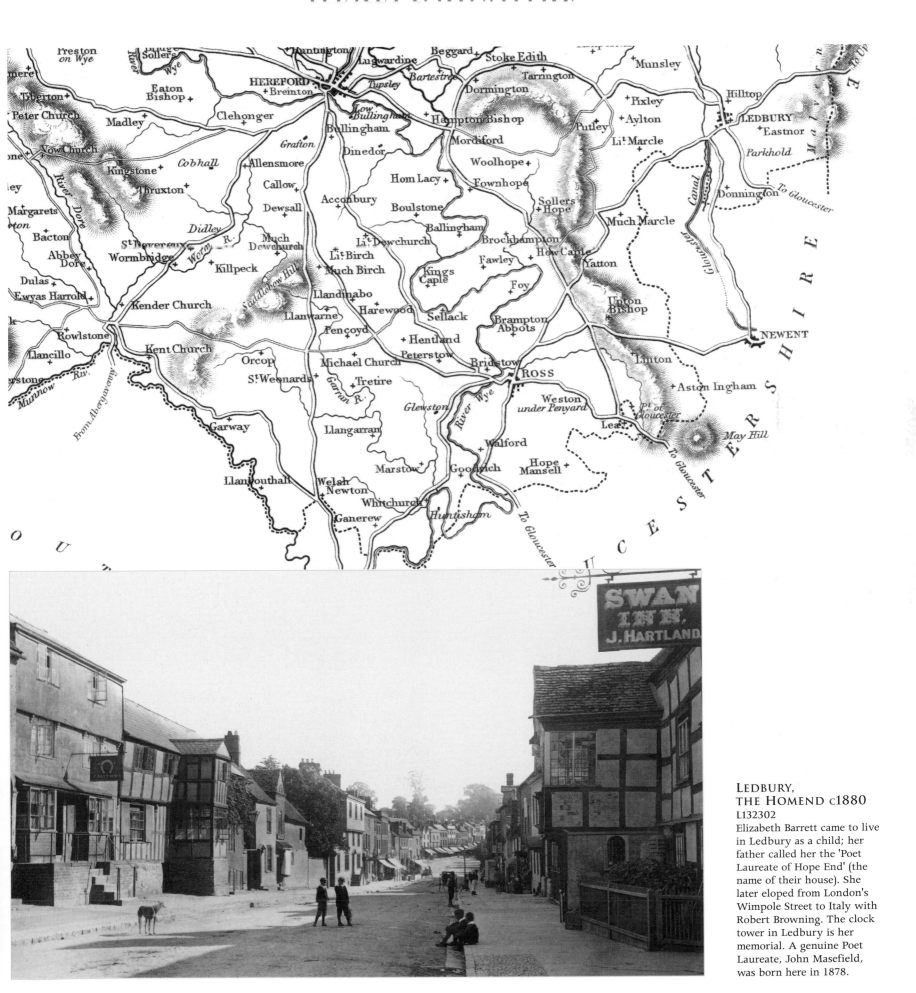

LEDBURY,
THE HOMEND c1880
L132302
Elizabeth Barrett came to live
in Ledbury as a child; her
father called her the 'Poet
Laureate of Hope End' (the
name of their house). She
later eloped from London's
Wimpole Street to Italy with
Robert Browning. The clock
tower in Ledbury is her
memorial. A genuine Poet
Laureate, John Masefield,
was born here in 1878.

worcestershire

Apart from those who know it well, the average traveller most often regards Worcestershire only from the speeding lanes of the M5 motorway, vaguely aware that the long line of hills rising dramatically to the west are the Malverns. But for the people who live and work in the surrounding countryside this is a county to be cherished, rich in historical importance and immortalised in English culture. Worcestershire is the county of Sir Edward Elgar, perhaps the nation's favourite composer, who found much inspiration in his native landscape. Bredon Hill is immortalised in the works of the poet A E Houseman, who lived most of his life in Bromsgrove, and the medieval poet William Langland also walked the Malvern Hills. Worcestershire also had its share of bloodshed - war between Henry III and the rebel barons under Simon de Montfort culminated in the murderous Battle of Evesham in 1265, the Welsh patriot Owain Glyndwr invaded in 1401, sacking and burning Worcester itself, and Worcestershire saw more than its share of the conflict of the Civil War. In more recent times the county has become a popular playground for thousands of visitors from the industrial conurbations of the Midlands, who seek out the Cotswolds, the Cathedral City of Worcester, and the boating rivers of the Stour and Severn.

WORCESTER, THE CROSS 1899 44010

The cathedral city of Worcester is situated almost in the centre of Worcestershire, on the banks of the River Severn. Worcester developed as a settlement in Saxon times, though it did not achieve importance as a city until after the Norman Conquest. Work started on the present cathedral in 1084. In the chancel, just before the high altar, is the tomb of King John, situated between the shrines of St Oswald and St Wulfstan. King John was particularly fond of Worcester and was buried in the cathedral at his own request. His tomb bears the first sculptured effigy in England, and is supposed to be a good likeness of the king.

STOURPORT-ON-SEVERN, THE BRIDGE 1904 51974
Stourport stands where the River Stour meets the Severn; it grew in importance after James Brindley built a canal junction here in the 1760s. The meeting of all these waterways proved important in the industrial development of the region. Brindley originally wanted to bring his canal to the Severn at Bewdley but the locals there objected to the very idea of such a 'stinking ditch'.

KIDDERMINSTER, THE CHURCH AND CANAL 1931 84619
The carpet industry began here in the 1700s. In later years both the River Stour and the associated canal systems were used to transport carpets on the first stage of their journeys to the market places of the world.

BEWDLEY, LOAD STREET 1931 84620
Leland was most impressed with Bewdley: 'The towne is set on the syd of a hill, so coningly that a man cannot wish to set a towne better...at the rysnge of the sunne from este the whole tow glittereth, being all of new building, as it were of gold'.

DROITWICH, HIGH STREET 1904 51938
Droitwich developed as a spa in the early 19th century thanks to John Corbett, a local businessman who opened the St Andrew's Brine Baths in the town for visitors, and built a magnificent French-style chateau just outside for himself. Towards the end of the 20th century the population increased when the town took some of the overspill from Birmingham.

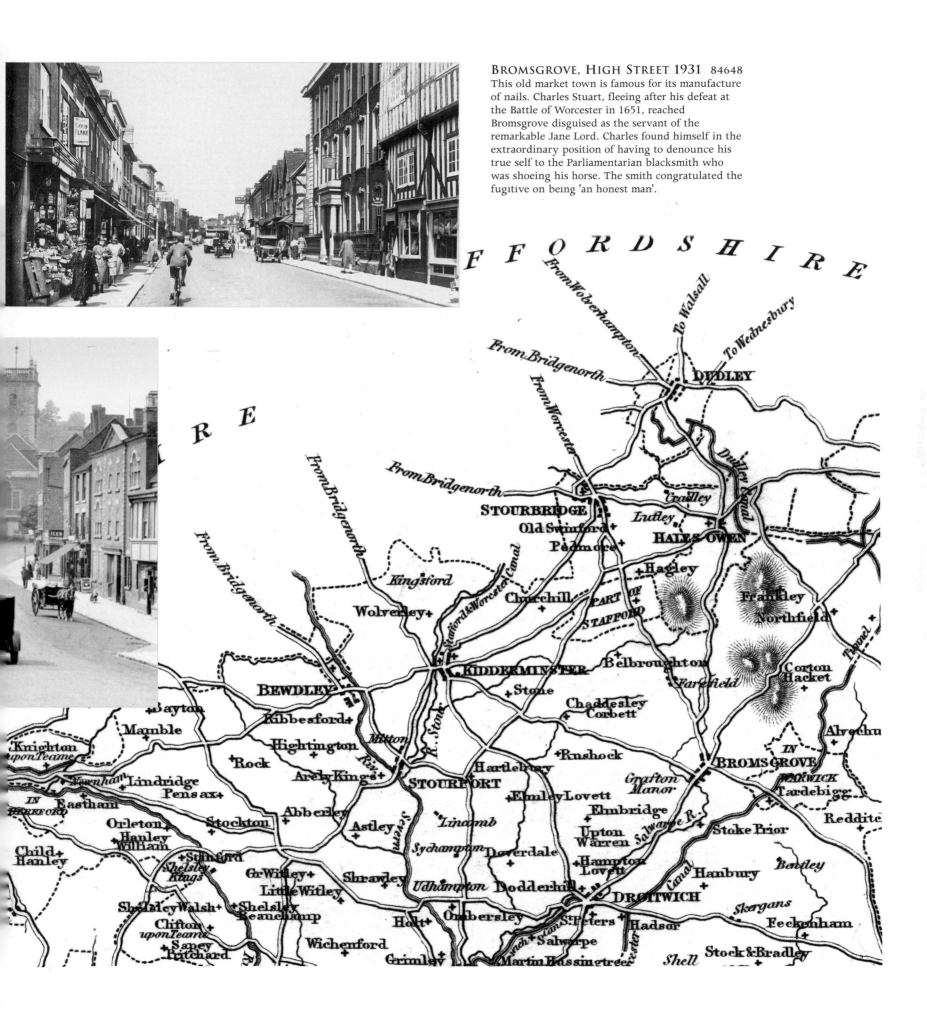

BROMSGROVE, HIGH STREET 1931 84648
This old market town is famous for its manufacture
of nails. Charles Stuart, fleeing after his defeat at
the Battle of Worcester in 1651, reached
Bromsgrove disguised as the servant of the
remarkable Jane Lord. Charles found himself in the
extraordinary position of having to denounce his
true self to the Parliamentarian blacksmith who
was shoeing his horse. The smith congratulated the
fugitive on being 'an honest man'.

WORCESTER, FRIAR STREET 1891 29321
Worcester was a walled city until the 18th century, and witnessed a great deal of conflict, particularly during the Civil War. Worcester's cathedral has many monuments to warriors from all periods in history, including the men of the Worcestershire Regiment who fell in 'the three glorious victories on the banks of the Sutlej in 1845 and 1846'.

UPTON UPON SEVERN, HIGH STREET 1931 84660A
In Upton's churchyard lies a landlord of the White Lion. His epitaph reads:

'Here lies the landlord of the Lion,
Who died in lively hopes of Zion;
His son keeps his business still,
Resigned unto the heavenly will.'

MALVERN WELLS, 1907 59029
The medicinal values of the waters around Malvern have been known for centuries. Holy Well was renowned for its treatment of people with eye problems. Dickens, Carlyle, Gladstone and Florence Nightingale all came to Malvern to 'take the cure'.

EVESHAM, HIGH STREET 1910 62339
At the centre of a broad vale, rich in market gardens and fruit orchards, and to which it gives its name, lies Evesham. However, during a thunderstorm on 4th August 1265, the Battle of Evesham was a scene of savage conflict between the forces of Henry III and the rebel barons of Simon de Montfort.

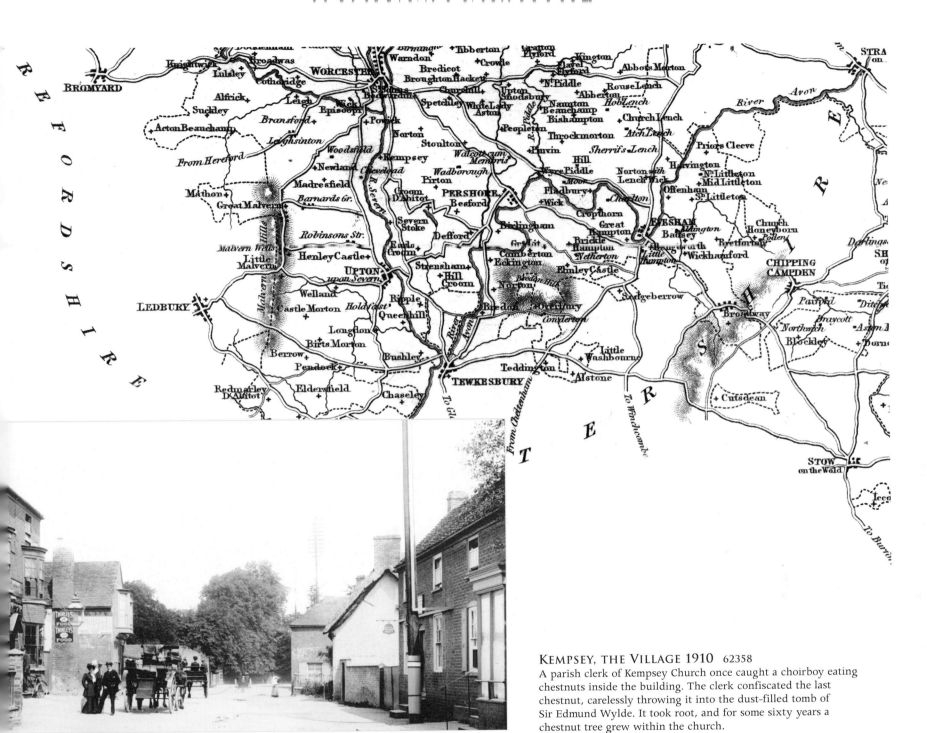

KEMPSEY, THE VILLAGE 1910 62358
A parish clerk of Kempsey Church once caught a choirboy eating chestnuts inside the building. The clerk confiscated the last chestnut, carelessly throwing it into the dust-filled tomb of Sir Edmund Wylde. It took root, and for some sixty years a chestnut tree grew within the church.

EVESHAM, BRIDGE STREET 1892 31106
A story tells how Eoves, the swineherd of Egwin, the Bishop of Worcester, saw a vision of the Virgin Mary in the meadows of the Avon. Egwin rushed to the spot and was told by Mary to found a monastery nearby. Evesham is reputedly named after Eoves the swineherd in commemoration of the event.

warwickshire

In 1974 local government reorganisation led to the creation of a number of large metropolitan boroughs. The West Midlands was created by taking up territory of Warwickshire and Staffordshire. Warwickshire lost its two great cathedral cities of Birmingham and Coventry, and with them the county's manufacturing and industrial heartland. With the decline of the Warwickshire coalfield the county was left with little in the way of industry, save for Nuneaton and Rugby. Agriculture was and is important, and many towns owed their early wealth to sheep and wool. The heart of present day Warwickshire is centred on Warwick itself, together with nearby Kenilworth, Leamington Spa and Stratford on Avon. In Kenilworth and Warwick are two of England's most famous castles: Kenilworth, a majestic ruin, and Warwick, a stately home second only to Windsor. For most people today Warwickshire is all about Stratford on Avon and William Shakespeare. Stratford is now the most visited literary shrine in the world.

WARWICK CASTLE FROM THE BRIDGE 1922 72366
The earliest fortifications at Warwick were thrown up in AD915 by order of Ethelfleda of Mercia, daughter of Alfred the Great. The ditch and palisade defences were placed around the town itself, Warwick at this time being little more than a frontier town next to the Danelaw. Ethelfleda joined with her brother Edward the Elder to reconquer English territory held by the Danes.

STRATFORD-UPON-AVON, THE MARKET PLACE 1892
31075
By the 14th century Stratford-upon-Avon was a prosperous market town noted for its annual Mop Fair, when farm workers would offer their services for the forthcoming year. Stratford's affairs were dominated by the Guild of the Holy Cross until the Guild's power was destroyed in 1547, when it was disbanded by order of Henry VIII. The town was then placed under the control of a bailiff; one holder of this office was none other than John Shakespeare, William's father. The Shakespeare connection has played an important part in the prosperity of Stratford, which is now England's premier tourist attraction outside London.

BIDFORD-ON-AVON, HIGH STREET 1899 44132
Bidford became famous in 1922 when a Saxon burial ground was discovered containing 200 graves, including those of warriors buried with their weapons.

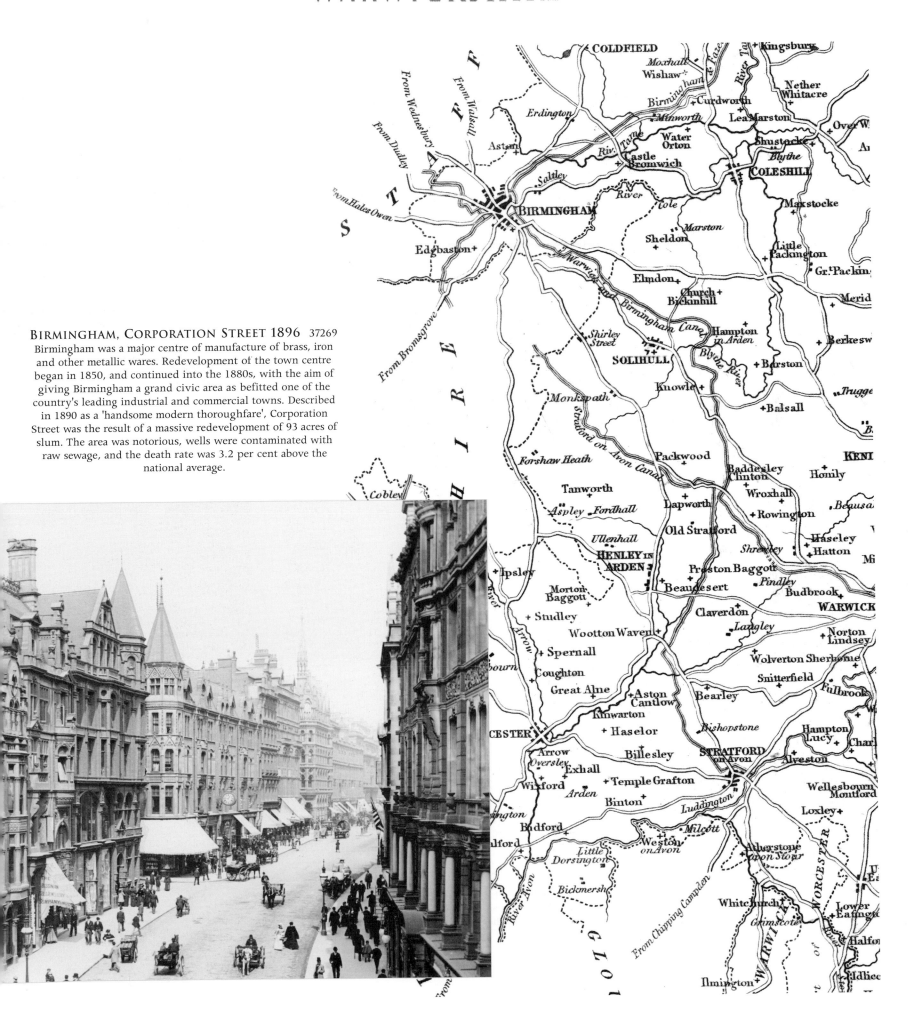

BIRMINGHAM, CORPORATION STREET 1896 37269
Birmingham was a major centre of manufacture of brass, iron and other metallic wares. Redevelopment of the town centre began in 1850, and continued into the 1880s, with the aim of giving Birmingham a grand civic area as befitted one of the country's leading industrial and commercial towns. Described in 1890 as a 'handsome modern thoroughfare', Corporation Street was the result of a massive redevelopment of 93 acres of slum. The area was notorious, wells were contaminated with raw sewage, and the death rate was 3.2 per cent above the national average.

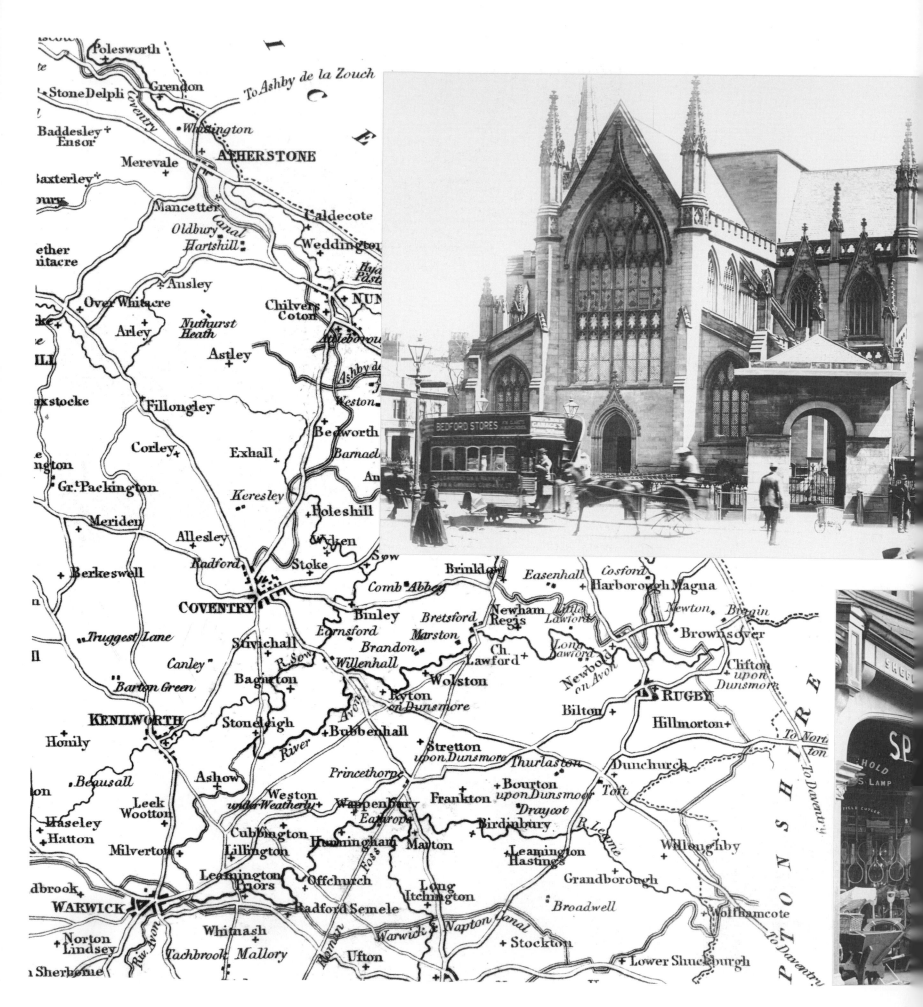

LEAMINGTON SPA, ALL SAINTS' CHURCH 1892 30961

In 1838 Queen Victoria came to drink the waters. She was received by Dr Henry Jephson, an outstanding surgeon in his day and also the man responsible for planning much of the town. It was Victoria who allowed the town to assume the name of Royal Leamington Spa.

WARWICK, ST JOHN'S 1892 31031

Though probably the least spoilt of all English county towns, little survives of pre-1694 Warwick. In that year much of the town centre was destroyed by fire.

KENILWORTH, THE VILLAGE 1892 30945

In 1906 it was possible to hire a horse and carriage at Warwick for a trip to Kenilworth and back for 10s 6d, though with 2 horses the price went up to £1, including the driver's fee. The castle ruins were the great attraction, especially after the success of Sir Walter Scott's novel 'Kenilworth', set during the period of the last building phase of the castle after 1563, when Elizabeth I gave it to her favourite, Robert Dudley, Earl of Leicester.

RUGBY, HIGH STREET 1922 72124

The founding of Rugby School in 1567 led to the town's growth. By the 1920's Rugby had become an important railway junction, and industrialisation came with the railways and the Oxford Canal. The town is also famous for 'the exploit of William Webb Ellis', a pupil of Rugby School who in 1823 carried the ball and ran instead of kicking it, in a soccer match.

leicestershire

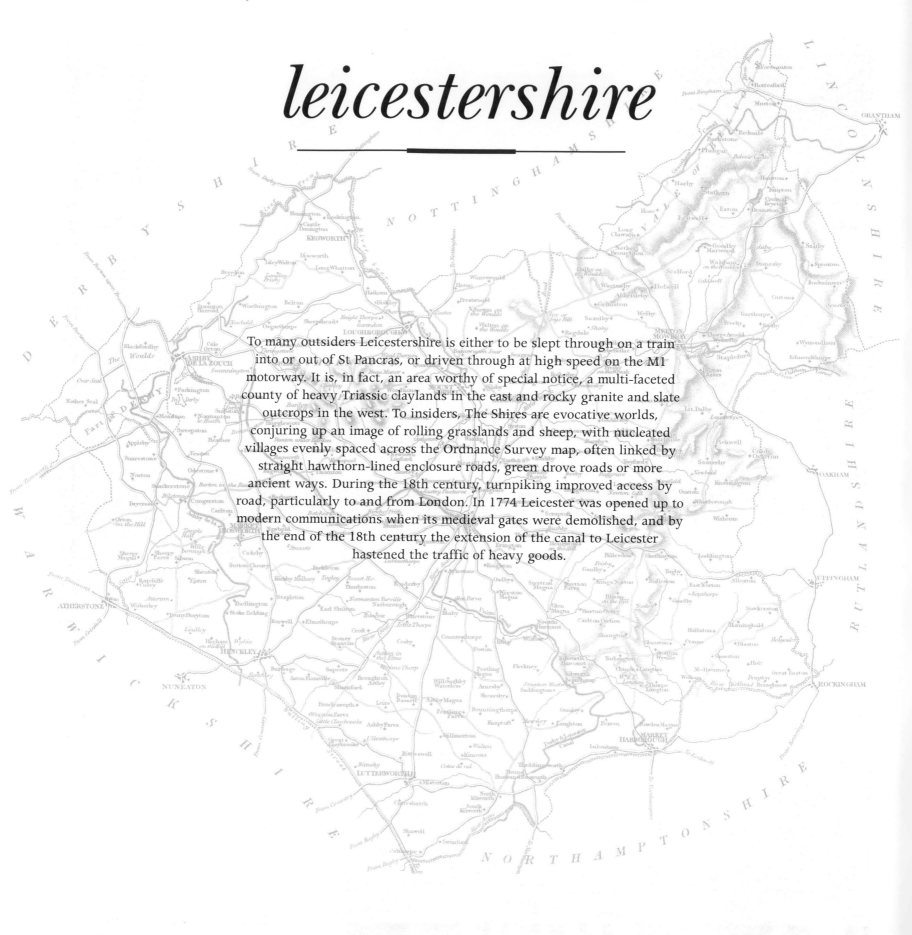

To many outsiders Leicestershire is either to be slept through on a train into or out of St Pancras, or driven through at high speed on the M1 motorway. It is, in fact, an area worthy of special notice, a multi-faceted county of heavy Triassic claylands in the east and rocky granite and slate outcrops in the west. To insiders, The Shires are evocative worlds, conjuring up an image of rolling grasslands and sheep, with nucleated villages evenly spaced across the Ordnance Survey map, often linked by straight hawthorn-lined enclosure roads, green drove roads or more ancient ways. During the 18th century, turnpiking improved access by road, particularly to and from London. In 1774 Leicester was opened up to modern communications when its medieval gates were demolished, and by the end of the 18th century the extension of the canal to Leicester hastened the traffic of heavy goods.

LEICESTER, BELGRAVE GATE 1949
L144015
Leicester grew rapidly in the 19th century; its hosiery industry flourished, aided by the successful boot and shoe and engineering industries. The greater part of the city consists mainly of 'Victorian' buildings, and Leicester has now become recognised as one of the great 19th century English cities.

MARKET HARBOROUGH, HIGH STREET 1922 72262
The town developed as a deliberately created market centre at the crossing of the River Welland; it was granted a weekly market in 1202. In the 18th century Market Harborough was little more than one great market street, but with the turnpiked road and the arrival of the Grand Union Canal along with the railways, industry began to settle in the town. Factories making carpets and footwear appeared close to the town, as did warehouses and a corn mill.

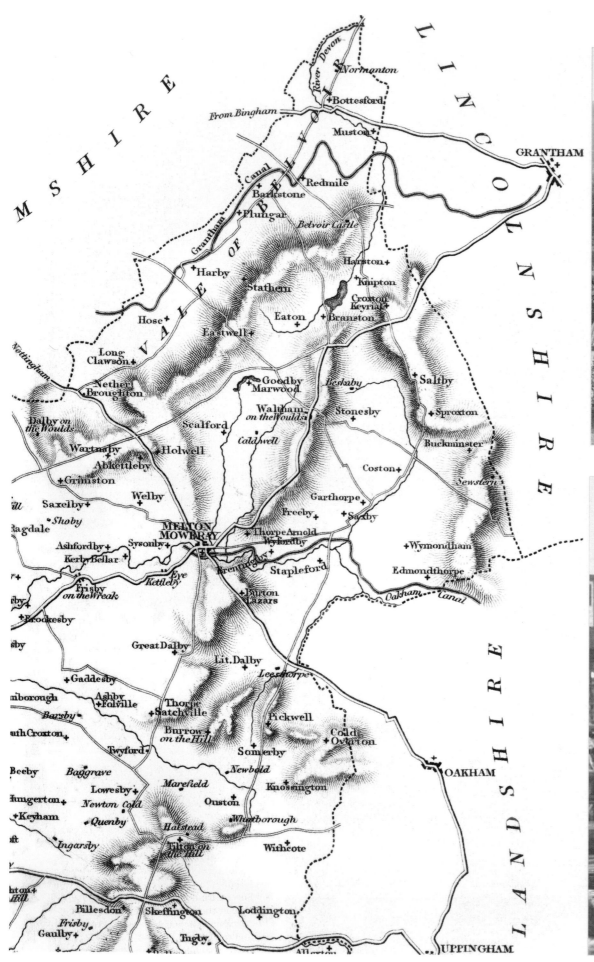

BELVOIR CASTLE 1890
27852
Belvoir Castle is picturesquely situated some six miles to the west of Grantham, at the foot of a narrow spur jutting up between Nottinghamshire and Lincolnshire. Prominent for miles around, it was built menacingly by William the Conqueror's standard-bearer, Robert de Todeni, on an escarpment rising some two hundred feet above the surrounding countryside.

MELTON MOWBRAY, MARKET PLACE 1932 85169
Melton Mowbray takes the second part of its name from the Norman lord Roger de Mowbray who lived here in about 1125. The town is the home of the world famous pork pie, which was probably created to feed hungry huntsmen as early as the 14th century. The recipe has changed over the years: the original contained currants, raisins and anchovies, as well as pork.

MELTON MOWBRAY, THE SHEEP MARKET c1955 M60027
Melton has been at the centre of the sheep farming industry for a number of centuries. Sheep farming in this area started from a time in the 15th century when the people of villages such as Ingarsby were ejected, and the more profitable sheep were moved in, by the monks of Leicester Abbey.

northamptonshire

Northamptonshire has long been a county through which major roads passed, radiating from London and the south, heading northwards. The first such road is the Roman Watling Street, bisecting the county from Old Stratford to Lilbourne. More recently, in the 1950s and early 1960s the M1 motorway fully integrated Northamptonshire into the country's main modern highway network. Northamptonshire has played a full part on the stage of British history. It was here that the Magna Carta barons met; Mary, Queen of Scots spent her last days at Fotheringay Castle, near Oundle, where she was executed in 1587; and the Battle of Naseby was a turning point in the first English Civil War, when Royalist forces were defeated by the Parliamentarian army. It was through Northamptonshire that Edward I travelled at the end of the 13th century, escorting the body of his beloved wife Eleanor from Lincoln to Westminster Abbey. The funeral cortege stopped twice in the county; Edward later marked the route of his journey with a series of ornate crosses. More than 700 years later, at the close of the 20th century, millions watched the final journey of Diana, Princess of Wales, as she was taken home to Althorp to be buried in the grounds of the great house.

KETTERING,
THE MARKET 1922 72233
Kettering had a booming
boot and shoe industry in
Victorian times, specialising
in heavy work boots.

NORTHAMPTON, GEORGE ROW 1922 72179

The growth of Northamptonshire's footwear manufacturing industries was influenced by two natural factors - lush grasslands and extensive forests.
The bark of oak trees provided the tanning materials, and the flocks and herds grazing on the grasslands the hides, for the leather. Over the years Northampton
acquired status as an important boot and shoe manufacturing centre, and shod most of Cromwell's army.

PETERBOROUGH, LONG CAUSEWAY 1904 51547
Now in modern Cambridgeshire, Peterborough's early riches were directly attributable to its monastery. Until the Dissolution, the Abbot exercised control over the local area, and sheep provided a handsome income. The monastery then became a cathedral, a special dispensation on the part of Henry VIII, whose first wife, Catherine of Aragon, was buried there.

GEDDINGTON, THE VILLAGE 1922 72253
Geddington is famous for its May Day tradition of distributing bread through the village. In the morning children take flowers to pensioners, then in the afternoon the May Queen is crowned on the steps of the cross.

PETERBOROUGH, COWGATE 1904 51559
Peterborough's magnificent 17th-century Guildhall is supported by columns to provide an open ground floor.

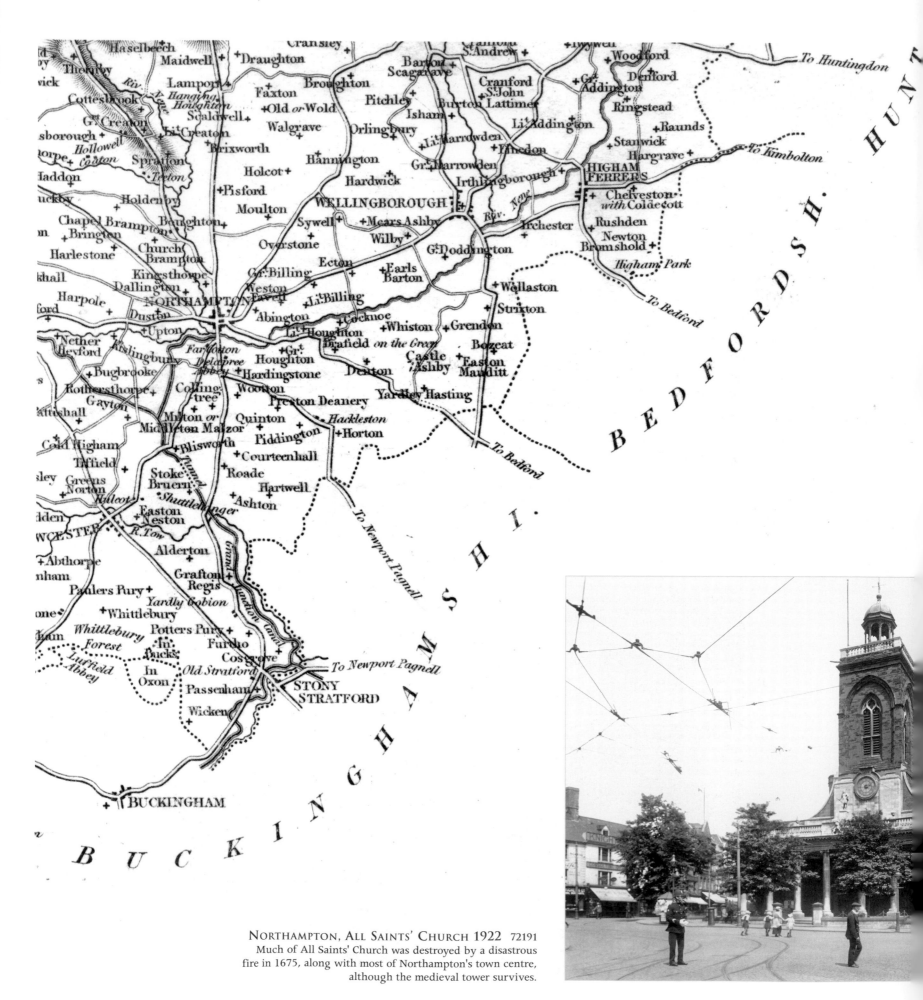

NORTHAMPTON, ALL SAINTS' CHURCH 1922 72191
Much of All Saints' Church was destroyed by a disastrous
fire in 1675, along with most of Northampton's town centre,
although the medieval tower survives.

KETTERING, THE MARKET 1922
72232
The grandeur of the west tower of
Saints Peter and Paul Church recalls the
sheep trade from which Kettering
gained its wealth in medieval times.

**NORTHAMPTON, FROM ALL SAINTS'
TOWER 1922** 72166
The River Nene flows through
Northampton: it has been an important
artery through the county for centuries.
One of its key roles was to provide cheap
and easy transport when roads were
difficult to negotiate. As a result, the
town's tanners and shoemakers set up
business along its banks.

huntingdonshire

Touring through Huntingdonshire is like taking a walk along a river bank. At every turn, the Great Ouse and its tributaries have scoured and moulded the landscape to the south and the east, whilst the Nene has shaped the countryside to the north and west. Being close to the Fens, any land routes have had to follow high ground. The Roman road known as Ermine Street may have followed the route of an Iron Age trackway, linking London and York, crossing the Great Ouse at Godmanchester and Huntingdon, and, further north, fording the Nene at Water Newton. The great towns of Huntingdon, Godmanchester, St Ives and St Neots based their prosperity on the river either as a roadway for transporting their produce or as a source of power for their developing industries.

HUNTINGDON, THE BRIDGE 1898 41251

The town of Huntingdon has strong associations with Oliver Cromwell, leader of the Parliamentarian forces during the Civil War and Lord Protector of England from 1653 until his death in 1658. He was born in the town, and educated at Huntingdon Grammar School. The medieval bridge over the River Ouse was started in 1332 to connect Huntingdon with Godmanchester, and the respective authorities paid for three arches, resulting in different styles, with the builders starting on each bank and meeting in the middle.

ST IVES, BRIDGE STREET 1914 66957
The first recorded wooden bridge in St Ives was built on the site of the original ford in
the early 12th century. The present bridge was constructed in Barnack stone in 1414.
During the Civil War, in 1645, one arch was removed and replaced with a drawbridge.

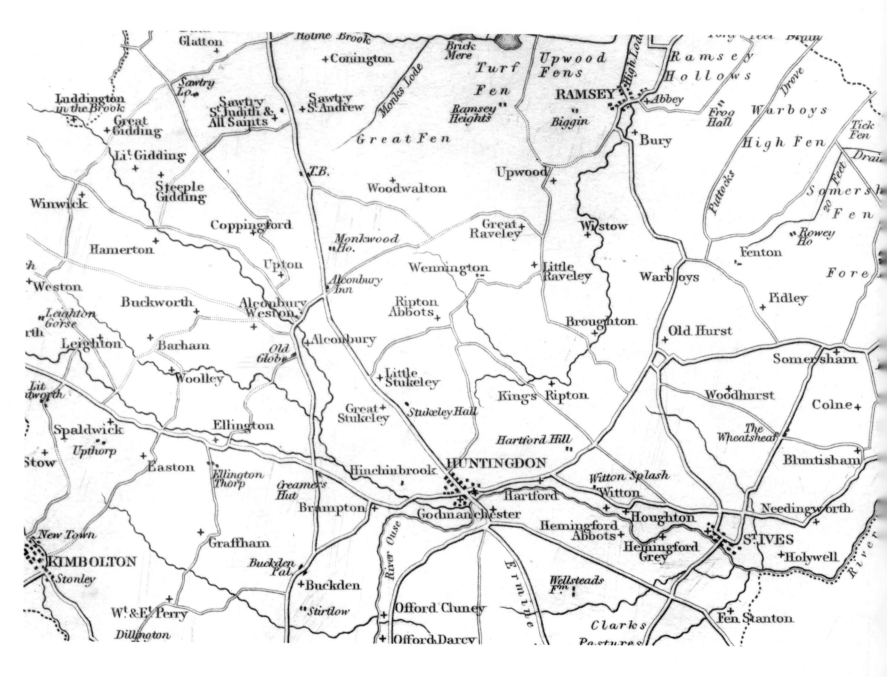

SPALDWICK, THE VILLAGE 1906
55433
Work on the tower and spire of
St James' Church in Spaldwick was
begun around the middle, but not
completed until the end of, the 14th
century. There is evidence that
building work slowed down about
half way up the tower, which may
possibly be indicative of labour
shortages caused by the Black Death.

ST IVES, MARKET HILL AND THE CHURCH 1901 48066
In the 17th and 18th centuries the quay at St Ives was a scene of bustling activity, with barges loading and unloading their cargoes. One of the town's famous oarsmen was John Goldie, the son of the Vicar. He was three times stroke for Cambridge in the Boat Race boat, and gave his name to the University's second boat.

ELLINGTON, THE VILLAGE 1906 55436
Ellington is recorded in the Domesday Book as having a population of about 150; the manor was held by the Abbot of St Benedict's, Ramsey. The chancel arch of the present church of All Saints' dates from the 13th century. The tower was built around 1390, and the nave arcades, north aisle and north porch were added shortly afterwards. During the 1860s Sir George Gilbert Scott redesigned and rebuilt the chancel.

bedfordshire

For millenia, that part of England that we identify as the English county of Bedfordshire has been a through-route to the rest of the Britain. Cattle, flint, salt, iron, implements and, latterly, goods from Gaul and the Mediterranean were traded across the country from Wessex to the Wash and back again via the route of the ancient Icknield Way. The Romans pushed three major routes north by strengthening and fortifying the existing Watling Street and Ermine Street ridge-bound ways; they used them to move the legions through Bedfordshire to the heavily fortified way line of the Fosse Way in Warwickshire and Lincolnshire. We know the same Roman roads today as the A5, the A6/A600 and the A1. The building of the waterways network in the 18th century brought the Grand Union Canal to the western edge of the county. In the 20th century the M1 motorway and Luton Airport have also been added to the county's transport system, and Bedfordshire was also home to the Vauxhall Motor Company, a major employer and producer of vehicles such as the Bedford van.

BEDFORD, HIGH STREET 1921 70425

Daniel Defoe described Bedford as 'a large populous, well built and thriving town'. The river was made navigable in the 1680s, and wharves, warehouses and stores appeared. Coal, fish brought up-river in perforated trunks towed behind the barges, salt, millstones, tar, iron, timber and bricks were landed at the wharves, while mainly agricultural produce such as what, malt, beans and apples in season were loaded for transport down river. Coal was the main import in the 18th century, and brewing grew in importance as an industry.

ELSTOW, THE VILLAGE 1897 39966
John Bunyan was born near Elstrow and made his adult home in the village. His tribulations and works, of which 'Pilgrim's Progress' is the best known, are celebrated in the establishment of the Bunyan Trail, a 75-mile long footpath which winds through the Bedfordshire countryside, linking elements of Pilgrim's journeys and the more factual elements of Bunyan's life.

AMPTHILL, THE MARKET PLACE c1955 A158030
Ampthill's history as a coaching stop is still visible in the form of the White Hart Hotel on the right of the picture.

BIGGLESWADE, HITCHIN STREET 1925 77217
Originally located on the Great North Road, Biggleswade was an important local market town. The Crown Hotel is believed to have been the source of the Great Fire of Biggleswade in 1785.

BEDFORD, HIGH STREET
1921 70423

First recorded as Bedanford in a document of AD880, the town was awarded borough status by Royal Charter in 1166. Bedford's importance is centred on its position astride the Great Ouse, at the confluence of the A6, the A600 and the A428 roads. The Town Bridge has long superseded the original ford, which was possibly guarded first by a Neolithic settlement, subsequently a Roman fort, then a Danish encampment, and finally by a Norman castle.

Scale of Miles

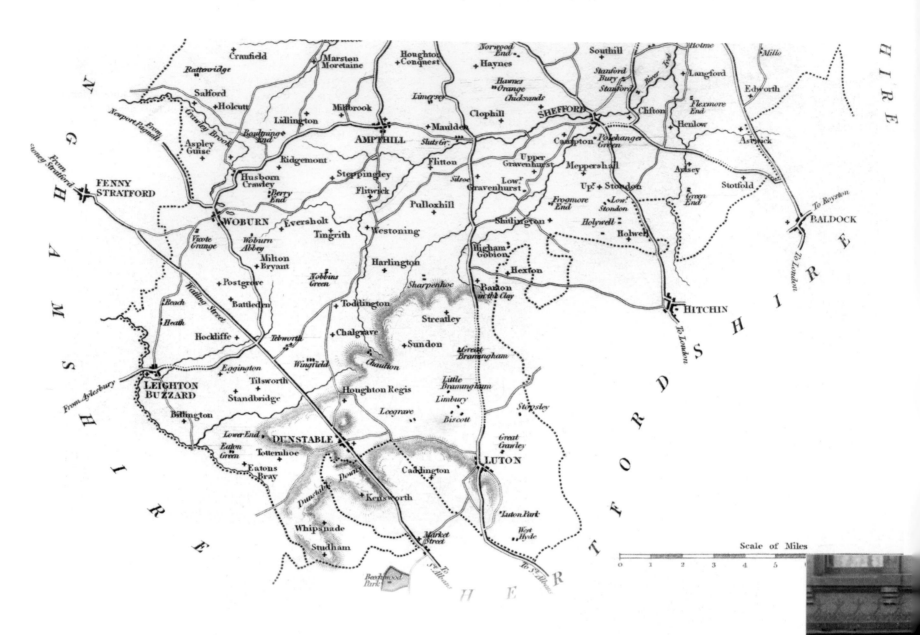

**TOTTERNHOE,
THE VILLAGE 1897**
39754
Totternhoe Knolls is the
name given to the
remains of Totternhoe
Castle, a motte and bailey
over Saxon remains, of
which only the ground-
works remain.

LUTON, GEORGE STREET 1897 39699

Luton was a centre of excellence of hat manufacturing. A large quantity of straw suitable for plaiting was used for boaters, panamas and even straw police helmets. In 1905 the Vauxhall Iron Works moved to Luton, and built cars for the wealthy and influential. The company was purchased by General Motors in 1925, to become Vauxhall Motors.

LEIGHTON BUZZARD, THE GRAND UNION CANAL c1955 L211049

The name Leighton Buzzard comes from a corruption of the Old English for a leek (or vegetable) farm, and Buzzard, an extension of the family name of Theobald de Busar, the first prebendary of the area. The Grand Union Canal (more properly called the Grand Junction) was intended to be the central artery of a web of canals linking London with Birmingham, the Potteries and the East Midlands.

LUTON, WELLINGTON STREET 1897 39704

Luton's original Town Hall, at the far end of George Street, was destroyed by fire during rioting after the Peace Day celebrations in 1919.

hertfordshire

Hertfordshire was originally one of the six smallest counties in England and Wales, yet the county incorporates a remarkable variety of landscape. To the north are vistas of rolling downland, and vast modern prairies of cereal crops. Farther east, where the Rivers Lea, Mimram and Stort wind through their courses, the ancient coppices and woodlands have been retained; the boulder clay topsoil encouraged the planting of barley, making this area the centre of the English malting industry. To the west lie the oak and beech woodlands of the Chilterns, while the southern sector of the county still boasts areas of cattle and sheep pastures amid the increasing swathe of new housing estates and industrial expansion.

During the 16th and 17th centuries many state officials, wealthy merchants, and bankers chose to live in Hertfordshire. They invested their riches in improving their properties and in adopting new farming techniques, as well as establishing a number of turnpike trusts to make the roads better. Later, the 18th-century navigational improvement of the Rivers Lea and Stort, and the building of the Grand Junction Canal brought the Industrial Revolution to the county. These innovations were followed by the advent of the railways, which by the late 19th century were to transform the county by allowing people to live in Hertfordshire and commute daily into London. The first main line to open was the London to Birmingham Railway from Euston, which reached Tring in 1837 though Watford and Berkhamstead. The Northern and Eastern Railway from Liverpool Street reached Broxbourne and Bishop's Stortford in 1842, and then moved on to Hatfield and Hitchin in 1850. The last of the main lines was the Midland Railway extension to London via Bedford, which enabled St Albans and Harpenden to join the Steam Age in 1868; finally the Metropolitan Railway extended to Rickmansworth and Chorleywood in 1889.

Where the railways went, housing developments quickly followed. The activities of the house-building arm of the Metropolitan Railway in particular, whose advertisements promoted the advantages of rural living combined with easy access for London, helped bring about the urbanisation of vast tracts of farmland in the south and west. During the last century the astonishing growth of motor transport has brought about even more radical changes. Britain's first six-lane motorway, the M1, which was opened in 1959, now cuts through the county from Brisley to Harpenden, whilst the vastly modified and expanded Great North Road, the A1M, extends from Barnet to Stortford. The massive road-building programme has also seen the creation of the London orbital M25 motorway, which curves through the southernmost reaches of Hertfordshire.

HERTFORD, FORE STREET 1922 71852

The county town of Hertford stands in a valley where three rivers meet. Its castle was besieged and captured by the French Dauphin in 1216, and later became a gaol for royal prisoners such as Margaret of Anjou, the wife of King Henry VI, King David of Scotland and King John of France. It was also a childhood home of Queen Elizabeth I. It has been suggested that Parliament may have met in Hertford in the 1500s during outbreaks of the plague in London. The Dimsdale Arms in Fore Street was named after the 18th-century doctor who innoculated Russia's Catherine the Great against smallpox.

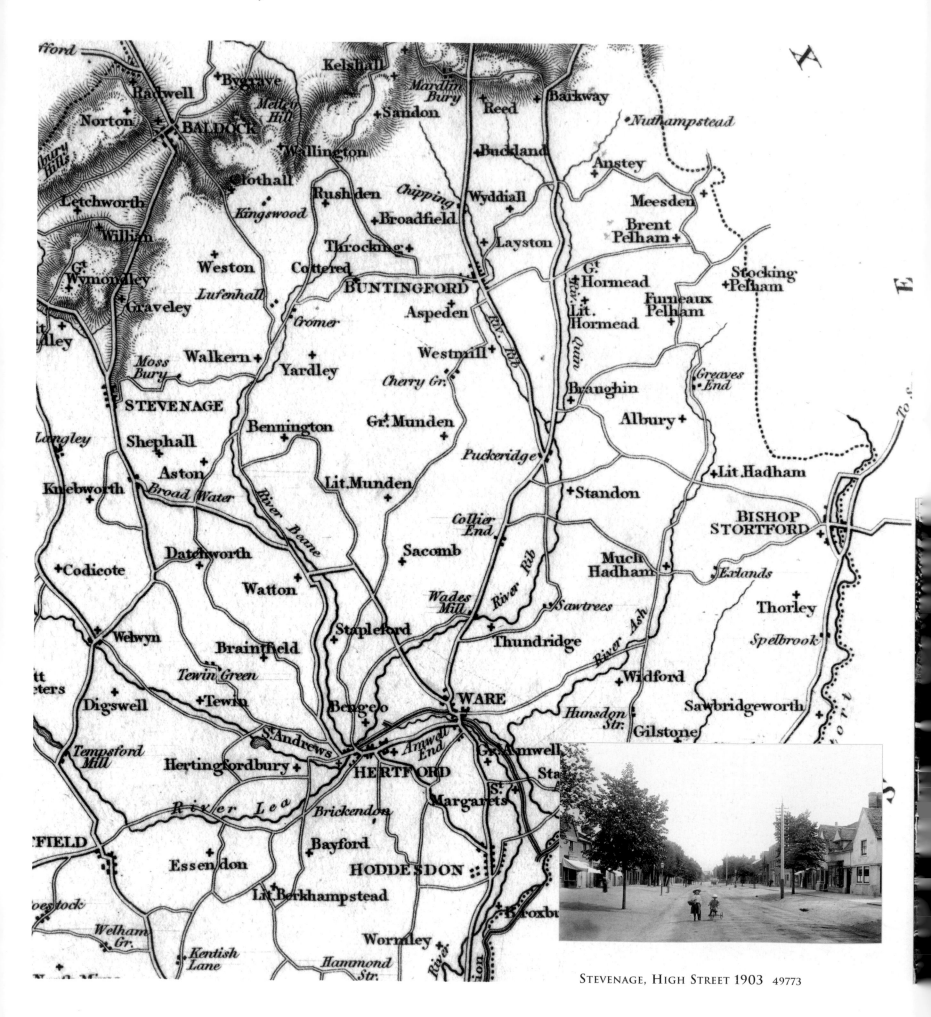

STEVENAGE, HIGH STREET 1903 49773

HERTFORDSHIRE

STEVENAGE, HIGH STREET AND THE GREEN 1899 44259
In the heyday of Stevenage, at the start of the 19th century, up to twenty stagecoaches a day passed along this stretch of the Great North Road. The town's wide High Street allowed the horse-drawn coaches to turn easily.

BISHOP'S STORTFORD, POTTER STREET 1903 49758
The production of malt was a major industry in Hertfordshire. At one time Bishop's Stortford had 17 maltings in the town. Barley and fuel for the furnaces were brought by water, and latterly by rail. Processing of the barley into malt took place from September to June; during this time the furnaces were never extinguished, and a sweet smelling pall covered the town. The sacks of malt and barley husks for cattle feed were loaded on to barges and transported to London.

BALDOCK, CHURCH STREET 1925 77100
Baldock's numerous inns made this small town one of Hertfordshire's premier coaching centres, thanks to its position on the Great North Road, and on the important link between Luton and Royston. Baldock's White Horse Street and Hitchin Street lie on the Icknield Way, a pre-Roman, Iron Age trading route running along the northern border of Hertfordshire.

HITCHIN, THE MARKET 1901
46633
The attractive old town of Hitchin has many fine buildings in a rich assortment of architectural styles, ranging from the 15th to the 21st centuries. The 12th-century tower and spire of St Mary's Church are a symbol of the medieval prosperity brought to the town by the wool trade. A famous son of Hitchin was Sir Henry Bessemer (1813-98), who revolutionised British industry with his invention in 1856 of the Bessemer Process for converting molten pig iron into steel.

ST ALBANS, HIGH STREET 1921 70476
Innumerable medieval pilgrims travelled to the town's abbey to worship at the shrine of St Alban. A Roman soldier named Alban, he was put to death around AD209 for sheltering a Christian priest, and was later canonised as Britain's first Christian martyr.

WATFORD, HIGH STREET 1921 70489
Watford's Holy Rood Catholic Church, built between 1883-90, was the inspiration of J F Bentley, later the architect of London's Westminster Cathedral.

cambridgeshire

The geology of Cambridgeshire ranges from sticky gault clays on the uplands to sand and gravel in the river valleys, with limestone outcrops and quarries in the north-west near Peterborough. Chalk and flints with clunch predominate to the south-west. Clunch is a form of chalk that was quarried around Burwell, Reach and Bassingbourne; it was easy to carve, and was particularly used for detailed work in medieval churches. Cambridgeshire and the former county of Huntingdonshire share a similar landscape of rolling hill country; small streams flow into the great river valleys of the Nene, Ouse and Cam, and then through the flood plains that become the wide expanses of fenland crossed by man-made drainage channels. The rivers brought invaders from Rome, Scandinavia and northern France. The Car Dyke and the original fen drainage channels, Ermine Street and the former road to Ely recently excavated at Landbeach, were all engineered by the Romans. Several ancient trackways cross over the county. The Icknield Way crossed the River Cam by parallel routes at the crossing points of Whittlesford, Duxford and Ickleton. Drovers used the ancient roads near the Great North Road to avoid tolls when it became turnpiked in 1662, and named them the Bullock Track. Causeways were built linking the fen islands; the earliest was at Andrett and was the ancient route to the Isle of Ely. Transportation of goods was usually by pack animals, on carts when seasonally possible, or by boats along the rivers and lodes. The rivers were the great highways between the market towns and river ports of Wisbech, Ely, Cambridge, St Ives, Huntingdon and St Neots.

CAMBRIDGE, CHRIST'S COLLEGE 1908 60831
Christ's College was founded in 1505 by Lady Margaret Beaufort, mother of Henry VII. The impressive gateway depicts her coat of arms, with
a statue of her above. In the college gardens stands a mulberry tree under which Milton is said to have written 'Lycidas'.

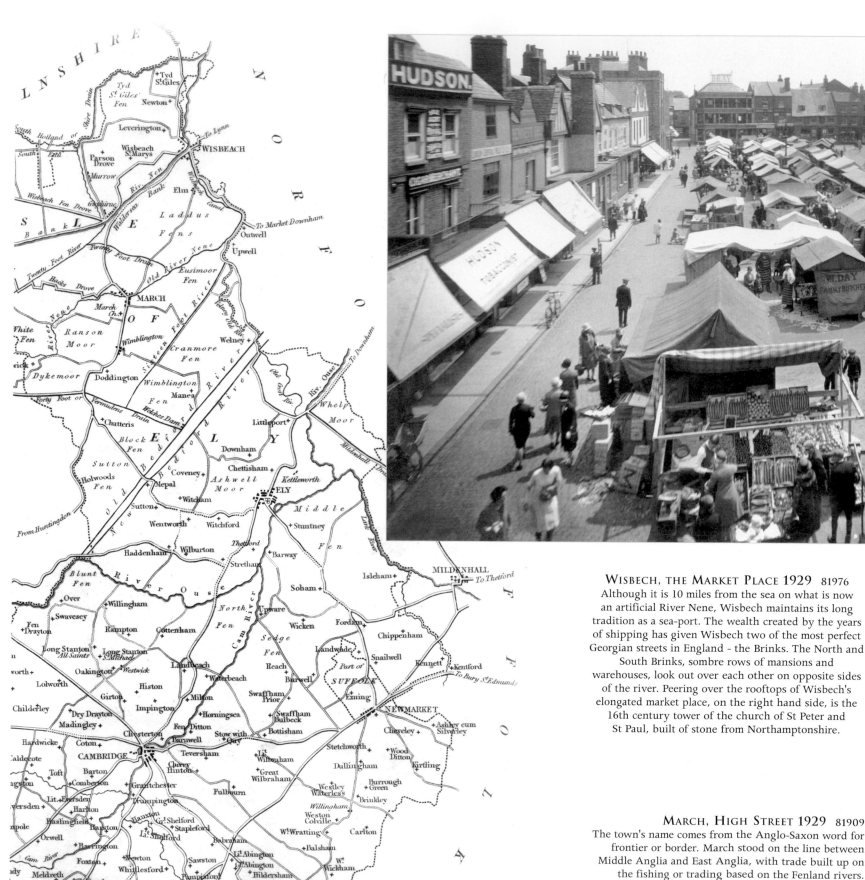

WISBECH, THE MARKET PLACE 1929 81976
Although it is 10 miles from the sea on what is now an artificial River Nene, Wisbech maintains its long tradition as a sea-port. The wealth created by the years of shipping has given Wisbech two of the most perfect Georgian streets in England - the Brinks. The North and South Brinks, sombre rows of mansions and warehouses, look out over each other on opposite sides of the river. Peering over the rooftops of Wisbech's elongated market place, on the right hand side, is the 16th century tower of the church of St Peter and St Paul, built of stone from Northamptonshire.

MARCH, HIGH STREET 1929 81909
The town's name comes from the Anglo-Saxon word for frontier or border. March stood on the line between Middle Anglia and East Anglia, with trade built up on the fishing or trading based on the Fenland rivers. By medieval times, March was a thriving town with an influence way beyond its bounds. The roof of St Wendreda's Church in March is a testament to the carpenter's art, a hammer beam roof with one hundred and twenty angels playing musical instruments.

LINTON, THE CHURCH c1955 L459076
Linton's timber-framed, jettied Guildhall faces the church. Dedicated to the Trinity, it was built
by parish subscription and a legacy from Nicholas Wickham in 1523. A serious fire in the village of Linton
was witnessed by Charles Darwin when he was a student.

CAMBRIDGE, PETTY CURY 1909 61469
Cambridge developed as a place of importance because of its position on the
Granta, or River Cam. It was at the head of a navigation and the only
crossing point for some considerable distance, hence Cam-bridge. The first
college to be founded, in 1284, was Peterhouse, by Hugh de Balsam, the
Bishop of Ely. Over the next couple of hundred years more colleges were
added, and their power grew. The University acquired the right to inspect
weights and measures in order that traders would not take advantage of the
students, which led to an uneasy relationship between 'town and gown'.

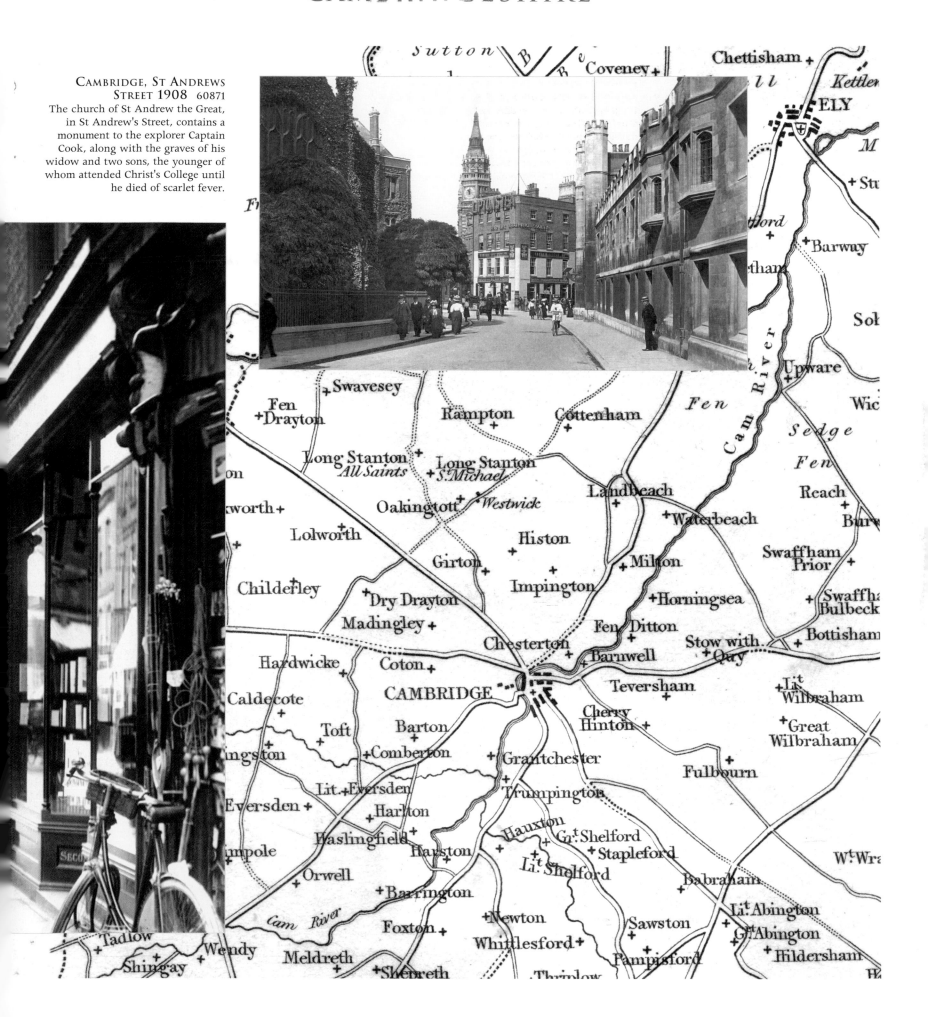

CAMBRIDGE, ST ANDREWS
STREET 1908 60871
The church of St Andrew the Great,
in St Andrew's Street, contains a
monument to the explorer Captain
Cook, along with the graves of his
widow and two sons, the younger of
whom attended Christ's College until
he died of scarlet fever.

essex

The image of Essex often presented is of a flat, rather dull place. This is completely underserved; Essex is steeped in history, with beautiful towns and villages, and some of the most notable churches to be found anywhere in England. The county covers 3,670 square kilometres (1,417 square miles). It is roughly square in shape, with its boundaries mainly defined by water: the River Stour to the north, the Rivers Stort and Lea (or Lee) to the west, the mighty Thames to the south, and the North Sea to the east. On the southern border, beside the River Thames, are the busy towns of Purfleet, Grays and the port of Tilbury. To the east lie the brooding ruins of Hadleigh Castle and the old fishing village of Leigh-on-Sea. Yet further along the coast comes the bustling brightness of Southend, with its famous pier stretching out into the estuary. Along the east coast, creeks and marshes have their own wild beauty; northwards is the major seaside town of Clacton, and yet further north lies the port of Harwich, now a gateway to the continent. Moving into the centre of the county we come to the large, busy towns of historic Colchester and the administrative centre of the county, Chelmsford. Then, too, there are the new towns of Basildon and Harlow. Because Colchester was of such importance in Roman Britain a good communications system was necessary, and a long straight road was built to link the town with London. Although the present-day A12 has been widened and altered, it follows much of the old route.

WALTON-ON-THE-NAZE 1891 29092
Walton-le-Soken was an agricultural and beachcombing parish that expanded into Walton-on-the-Naze in the 1820s. Its early visitors were upper-class people who had summer homes here. The arrival of the railway in 1867, and the 1872 National Bank Holiday Act, opened Walton up to everybody.

CHELMSFORD, HIGH STREET 1895 35514

Chelmsford is the administrative centre of Essex, and has had its own cathedral since 1913. Its livestock market, which began about AD1200, is one of the most important in the area. Chelmsford was the location of the world's first radio factory, set up in 1899 by Gugliemo Marconi in Hall Street. The factory was later moved to New Street, and Britain's first radio programmes were transmitted in 1920.

SAFFRON WALDEN, HIGH STREET 1919
69134
Saffron Walden is named after the saffron crocus, which was used for dying woollen cloth here in the Middle Ages, when the town was prosperous and important in the wool trade. The town boasts a maze that dates back to prehistoric times.

ROMFORD, SOUTH STREET 1908 59808
Colonel Blood lived in Romford for three years whilst he planned his daring theft of the Crown Jewels from the Tower of London in 1671. When the jewels were returned Charles II gave Blood a pardon, a pension and an estate in Ireland.

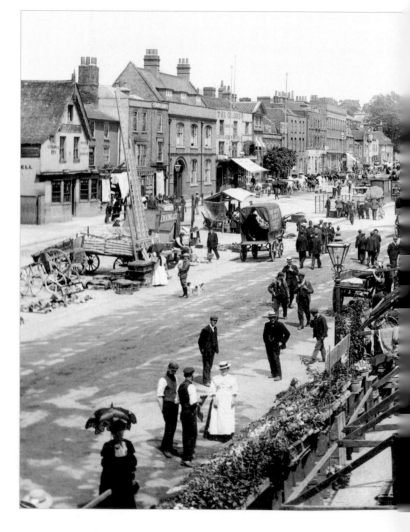

ROMFORD, THE MARKET 1908 59811
In 1247 King Henry III granted Romford a charter permitting a livestock market to be held in the town every Wednesday. It provided a centre on the Essex Great Road where sheep and cattle farmers could sell their stock. The Wednesday cattle market continued for over 700 years, the final one being held in 1958.

EPPING, HIGH STREET 1921 70132
Close by Epping is Epping Forest, a favourite place for family outings
and picnics. This is but a small remnant of the ancient Forest of Epping
that existed in pre-historic times. Both Henry VIII and Elizabeth I
hunted here. In 1882 Queen Victoria announced that the forest
should be for the use and enjoyment of her people for all time.

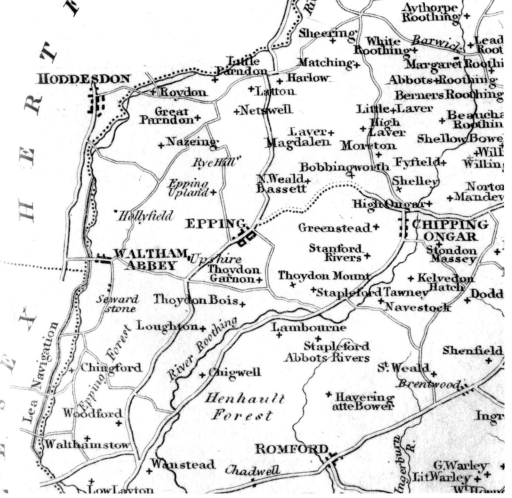

BRAINTREE, HIGH STREET 1906 55533
The prosperity of Braintree has developed from agriculture,
brush making and textiles. At first the trade was in woollen cloth, but in the
19th century the Courtauld family introduced silk weaving to the town.

CLACTON-ON-SEA, FROM THE JETTY 1912 64252

Although Great Clacton was long established as a medieval market village, the seaside town did not really develop until the 1870s. The pier was built in 1873, and lengthened in the 1890s to 1,180 feet. By the years just before the Second World War it had become a thriving town attracting many holiday visitors.

COLCHESTER, HIGH STREET AND TOWN HALL 1901 47650

Colchester - still marketed as 'Britain's oldest recorded town' - had been a tribal capital before the Romans arrived. The Romans made it an administrative centre of their own, and the town is still scattered with Roman remains, despite Boudicca's attempts to raze the place to the ground. The High Street lies along the central axis of the Roman legionary fortress, and the town is still dominated by an important garrison in the 21st century.

suffolk

Suffolk has some 50 miles of coastline, much of it with beautiful heaths as its hinterland. Over the centuries the shape of the coastline has changed considerably. Towns like Aldeburgh, Dunwich and Covehithe have all suffered from erosion. Elsewhere the coastline has built up: Orford, for example, was once open to the sea, and is now separated from it by a long spit of shingle formed by a process called longshore drift. Over the centuries a number of different industries have kept Suffolk prosperous. In medieval times the backbone of industry in the area was the wool and cloth-weaving trade. Many Dutch and Flemish weavers settled here when sheep farming was at its height, and created a wool industry which became world-famous. As a result, many buildings in East Anglia have a pronounced Dutch influence. At the peak of the industry, before the Industrial Revolution of the late 18th century moved the textile industry to the Pennines, Suffolk was producing more wool than any other county in England, and local variations of heavy broadcloth was exported all over Europe. Suffolk also had a thriving fishing industry, in particular the herring trade. The coming of the railway in the 19th century undoubtedly changed the face of the region. Although the sailing barges which carried goods up and down the east coast carried on into the early 20th century, the trains started to eat into their business. But the biggest change came simply with the movement of people. Towns like Lowestoft and Felixstowe became tourist resorts, and many developments rapidly followed.

IPSWICH, BUTTER MARKET 1893 32204
The county town of Suffolk, Ipswich was granted its first charter by King John in 1200. It was a busy medieval port, serving the Continental cloth trade.
It is still a busy port today, handling over two and a half million tons of cargo each year.

SUDBURY, MARKET 1904 51156
Sudbury was once the largest of the East Anglian woollen centres. The artist Thomas Gainsborough was born in here in 1727, in a former 16th-century inn, and he lived and worked in the town for a number of years.

BURY ST EDMUNDS, CORNHILL 1898
41246
The motto of Bury St Edmunds is ' shrine of a King, cradle of the law', referring to two major events in the town's history: the bones of the martyred Saxon king, St Edmund, were interred in the local monastery 33 years after his murder by the Danes in AD870; and in 1214 the English barons met here to swear to force King John to accept Magna Carta.

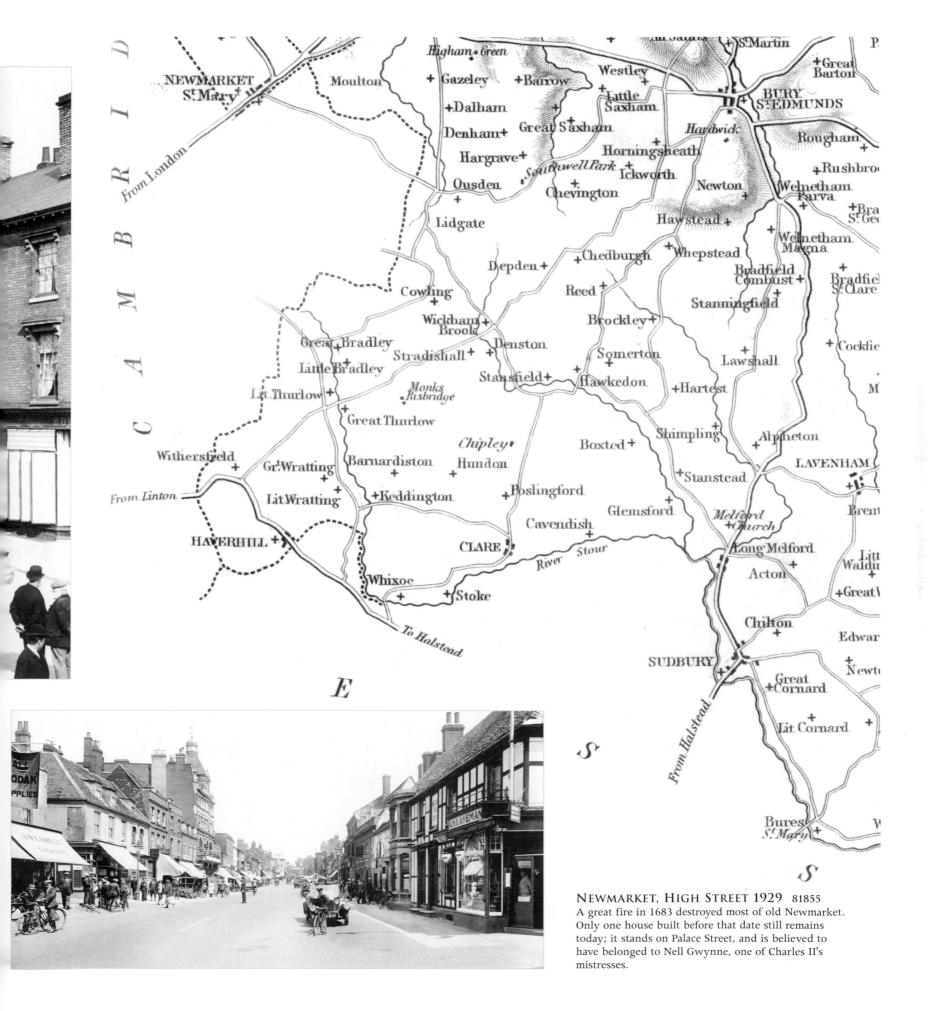

NEWMARKET, HIGH STREET 1929 81855
A great fire in 1683 destroyed most of old Newmarket.
Only one house built before that date still remains
today; it stands on Palace Street, and is believed to
have belonged to Nell Gwynne, one of Charles II's
mistresses.

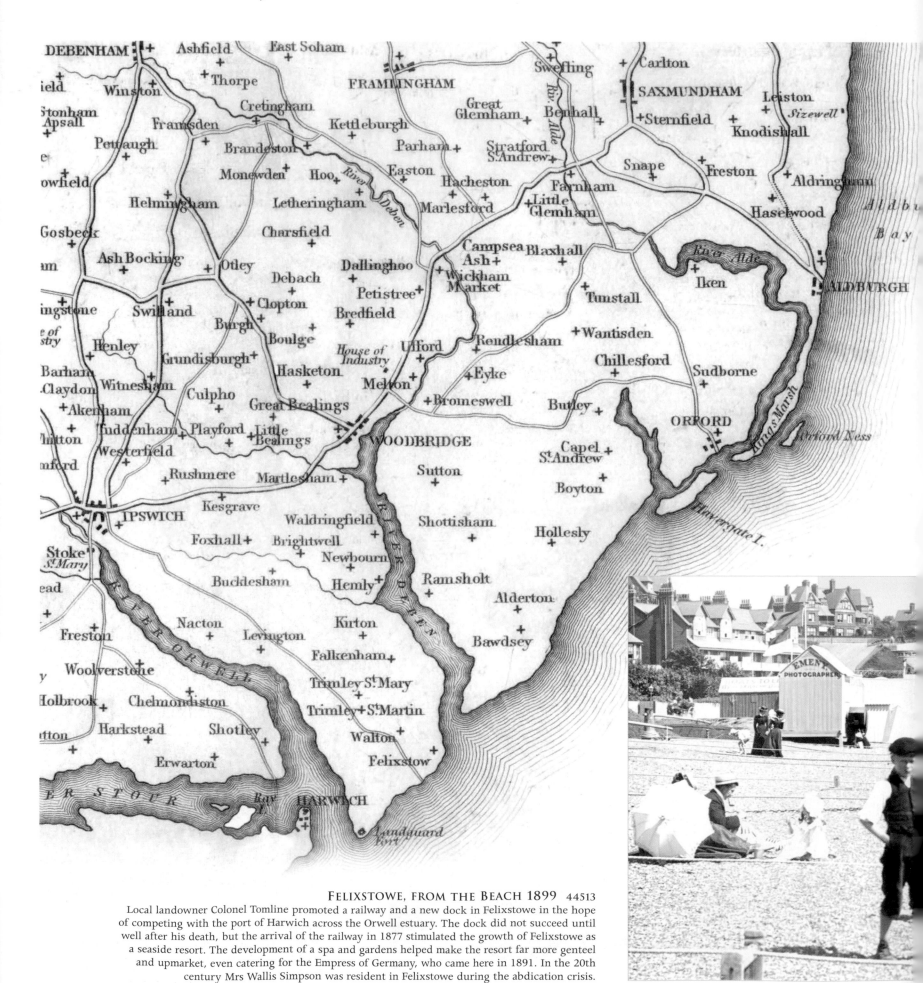

FELIXSTOWE, FROM THE BEACH 1899 44513
Local landowner Colonel Tomline promoted a railway and a new dock in Felixstowe in the hope
of competing with the port of Harwich across the Orwell estuary. The dock did not succeed until
well after his death, but the arrival of the railway in 1877 stimulated the growth of Felixstowe as
a seaside resort. The development of a spa and gardens helped make the resort far more genteel
and upmarket, even catering for the Empress of Germany, who came here in 1891. In the 20th
century Mrs Wallis Simpson was resident in Felixstowe during the abdication crisis.

IPSWICH, THE DOCKS 1893 32208

At the head of the Orwell estuary, Ipswich has been a major port for centuries. The Wet Dock (which made part of the port non-tidal) was constructed between 1839 and 1842, and at the time it was the most revolutionary and biggest of any kind in the country. Outside the Wet Dock, tidal moorings were built for larger ships.

LEISTON, SIZEWELL ROAD 1922 72579

Much of Leiston is a model village constructed by the Garrett family; they owned the Leiston Iron Works, where Richard Garrett produced a famous portable steam engine and threshing machine.

norfolk

Norfolk is almost an island: two sides are bordered by the North Sea, while the western boundary runs virtually beside the River Great Ouse, which flows into the Wash at King's Lynn. Only a few yards from the Ouse is the source of the Waveney, which flows eastwards, forming the boundary with Suffolk and coming out into the sea at Great Yarmouth. The west of Norfolk south of King's Lynn is fenland, and the marshes were virtually impassable before the Romans began to drain them. The dykes fell into disrepair when the Romans legions departed in the fifth century; Norfolk again became isolated, until 18th-century engineers initiated a massive system of drains and sluices, which nowadays controls the flow of water as far as the Midlands and the London area. Villages in Norfolk have grown out of settlements wherever a living could be made, and are usually sited on locally high ground and near water. Many have developed along a droving lane which has become a main highway. These linear villages, such as Long Stratton, Horsford and Watton, usually have a wide main street, a relic of the days when cattle and sheep were driven through. However, the most important transport links in the county were by water. Goods from Europe were off-loaded at Yarmouth and put on to wherries, the flat-bottomed, broad-beamed boats with black sails that are often seen in pictures of Norfolk life. The main trade was up the Yare to Norwich, but the other rivers were busy too. Where the rivers were too shallow, they began to be canalised, allowing wherries to travel further upstream. The first railway in Norfolk ran from Yarmouth to Norwich, opening in 1844, and over the next 50 years the railway reached every town in Norfolk and many villages too - at the peak of the railway age there were over 150 stations in the county. Trains took Norfolk produce such as turkeys and herrings to London, and also opened up the county to visitors from the cities, developing the holiday trade on which Norfolk has increasingly come to depend.

NORWICH, ROYAL HOTEL AND POST OFFICE 1901 46672

There is a spacious air about Norwich, the capital of Norfolk and 'city of churches'. At its heart are a great cattle market and two magnificent buildings, the cathedral and the castle, both Norman in origin. Parts of its old medieval walls are still standing, and this deepens its atmosphere of history and tradition.

ACLE, THE GREEN FROM THE POST OFFICE c1925 A204004

Acle is a busy market town, one of the early possessions of the Bigod's, who founded a priory here during the reign of Edward I.

**HUNSTANTON,
THE GREEN AND THE PIER
1907** 58895
Hunstanton is unique for north Norfolk resort towns in that it looks west across the sea and not east. It was a quiet village of simple fishermen's cottages until the coming of the railway in 1862. Then building began in earnest as visitors flocked to enjoy its safe, sandy beach and bracing cliff-top walks.

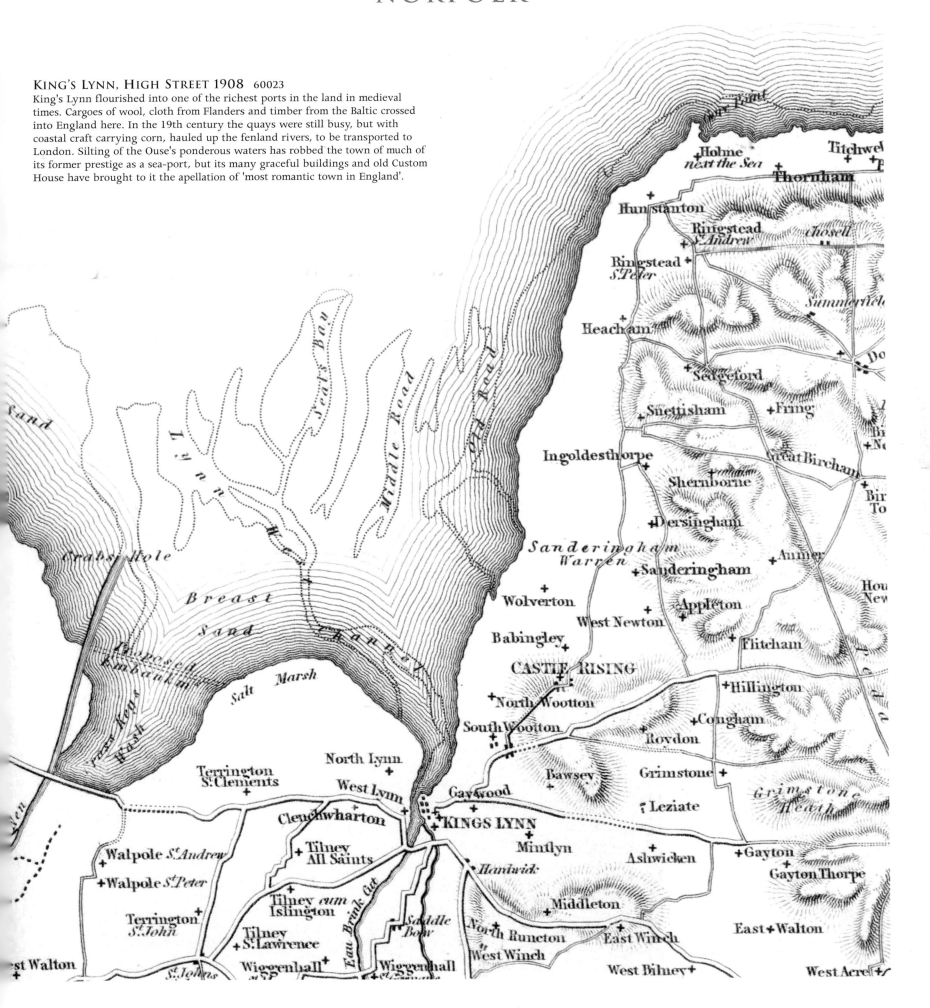

KING'S LYNN, HIGH STREET 1908 60023

King's Lynn flourished into one of the richest ports in the land in medieval
times. Cargoes of wool, cloth from Flanders and timber from the Baltic crossed
into England here. In the 19th century the quays were still busy, but with
coastal craft carrying corn, hauled up the fenland rivers, to be transported to
London. Silting of the Ouse's ponderous waters has robbed the town of much of
its former prestige as a sea-port, but its many graceful buildings and old Custom
House have brought to it the apellation of 'most romantic town in England'.

GREAT YARMOUTH, THE AMUSEMENT PARK, BRITANNIA PIER 1908
60647

This celebrated east coast resort has been a flourishing fishing port since the early Middle Ages. For centuries it suffered continual silting. By the 16th century the old river channel had become so blocked with sandbanks that the town burghers had to enlist the help of Dutch engineers to cut a new river mouth.

COLTISHALL,
A CORNFIELD 1902
48127
Coltishall still borders the
River Bure and marks the end
of the navigable waterway
up from Yarmouth. It is set
amid gently rolling, rich
agricultural land where the
main crops are corn and
sugar beet.

CROMER, THE SANDS
1899 44485
Set high above the sea, but
sheltered by wooded hills,
Cromer was once little more
than a jumble of simple
cottages huddled around the
church, and the exclusive
haunt of fishermen and
crabbers. The town
burgeoned into a popular
resort with the coming of the
railways. Only Yarmouth
attracts more visitors.

lincolnshire

After the end of the Roman occupation the area now known as Lincolnshire became a political entity for the first time as the Anglian Kingdom of Lindsey; the kingdom was absorbed into Mercia not long after AD700. Being on the east coast, and with the Trent and Witham highly navigable, the area was highly vulnerable to the longship-borne marauding armies of Danes, who are first recorded in the Chronicles as ravaging the area in AD839. Subsequently there was considerable Danish settlement; hundreds of Danish place-names can be found, particularly in the northern two-thirds of Lincolnshire. Place names ending in -by, -toft, -thorpe, and -ness, for example, abound. After Guthrum's peace with Alfred the Great in AD886, which created the Danelaw, the whole of eastern Mercia, including its province of Lindsey, was ruled by armies based in the Five Boroughs: Stamford and Lincoln were two of them, Derby, Leicester and Nottingham the other three. Although Lincolnshire was reconquered by the English by AD920, the Danish left an indelible imprint, together with large numbers of settlers who changed the ethnic mix for ever. Indeed, in 1013-14 Gainsborough was England's capital - Sweyn Forkbeard received the submission of the English rulers here. Sweyn died in Gainsborough on 2nd February 1014, and his son, the famous King Canute, subsequently ruled the whole of England.

BOSTON, MARKET PLACE 1899 43295
Boston, Botolph's Town, was granted its first charter by King John in 1205. It became a major centre of the wool trade. The town centre is dominated by its very large triangular market place, which in turn is overwhelmed by the mighty church steeple, completed in 1460 and universally known as the Boston Stump.

LINCOLN, STONEBOW 1901 46773

Lincoln is situated where the River Witham cuts through a limestone ridge. Medieval Lincoln expanded from the Roman walled town southwards along the Roman Ermine Street. Famous for its Norman castle and medieval cathedral, Lincoln also boasts the oldest canal in the country: the 11 mile long Fossdyke Navigation, dug by the Romans more than 1,800 years ago and still in use.

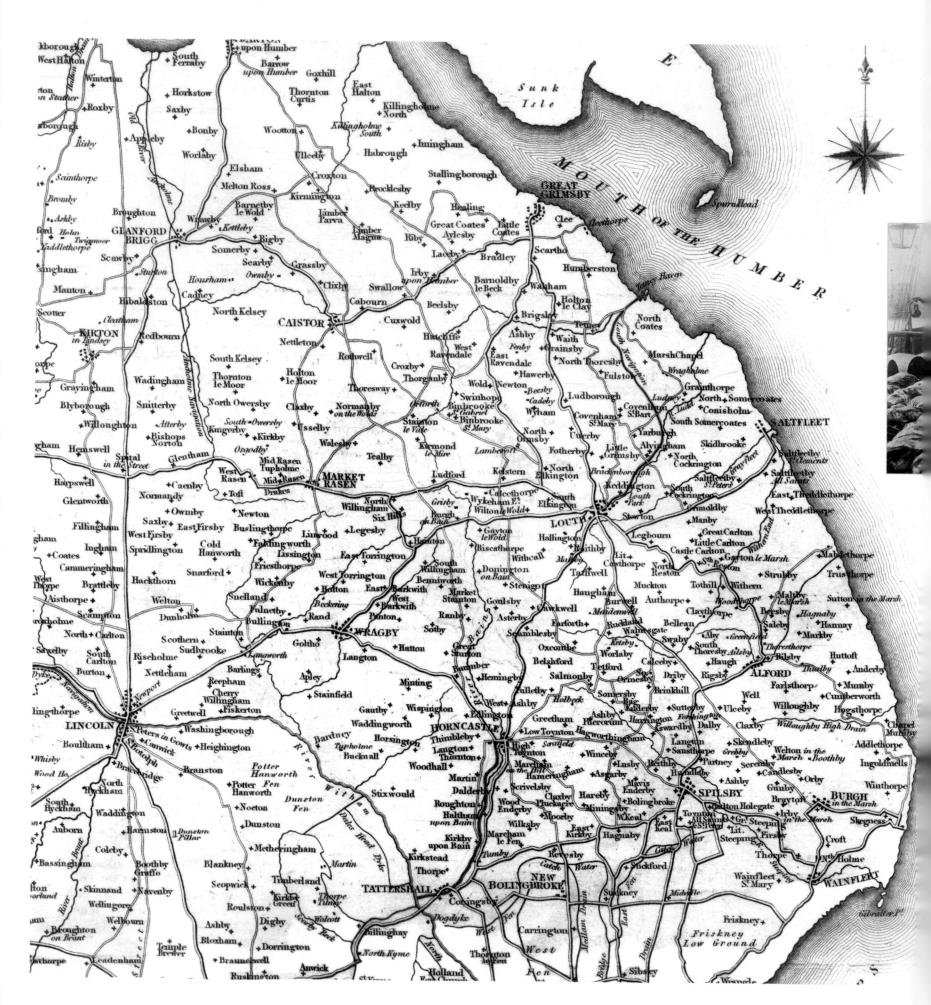

GRIMSBY, THE FISH PONTOON 1906 55748

In its day Grimsby was the biggest fishing port in the world, but it has been much diminished since the Icelandic waters were closed to British fishing fleets. Grimsby's Dock Tower was opened by Queen Victoria and Prince Albert in 1855. It was built as an hydraulic accumulator to control the water pressure to enable the dock's gates to be opened and closed; it also supplied power to the 15 working cranes. Electricity has now taken over its original function, but the Tower still stands proudly high above the docks.

MABLETHORPE, MAIN STREET 1890 26717

Mablethorpe developed as a seaside resort after the railway arrived in 1877. At very low tides, the remnants of tree stumps can be seen, all that is now left of a village and forest that was engulfed by the sea in 1289.

LINCOLN, THE CATHEDRAL AND STONEBOW 1890 25654

Lincoln's celebrated Stonebow is the later 15th-century medieval gate into the walled town, above which is the basically Tudor Guildhall of the city.

MARKET DEEPING, MARKET PLACE 1900
M116301
The large, triangular market place of Market Deeping was lined with coaching inns for travellers.

STAMFORD, MARKET PLACE 1922 72298
One of England's most attractive and historic towns, Stamford is only just in Lincolnshire. The River Welland is the boundary between it and Northamptonshire. The town would have looked very different to a late medieval traveller, when there were 14 parish church towers to be seen against the skyline.

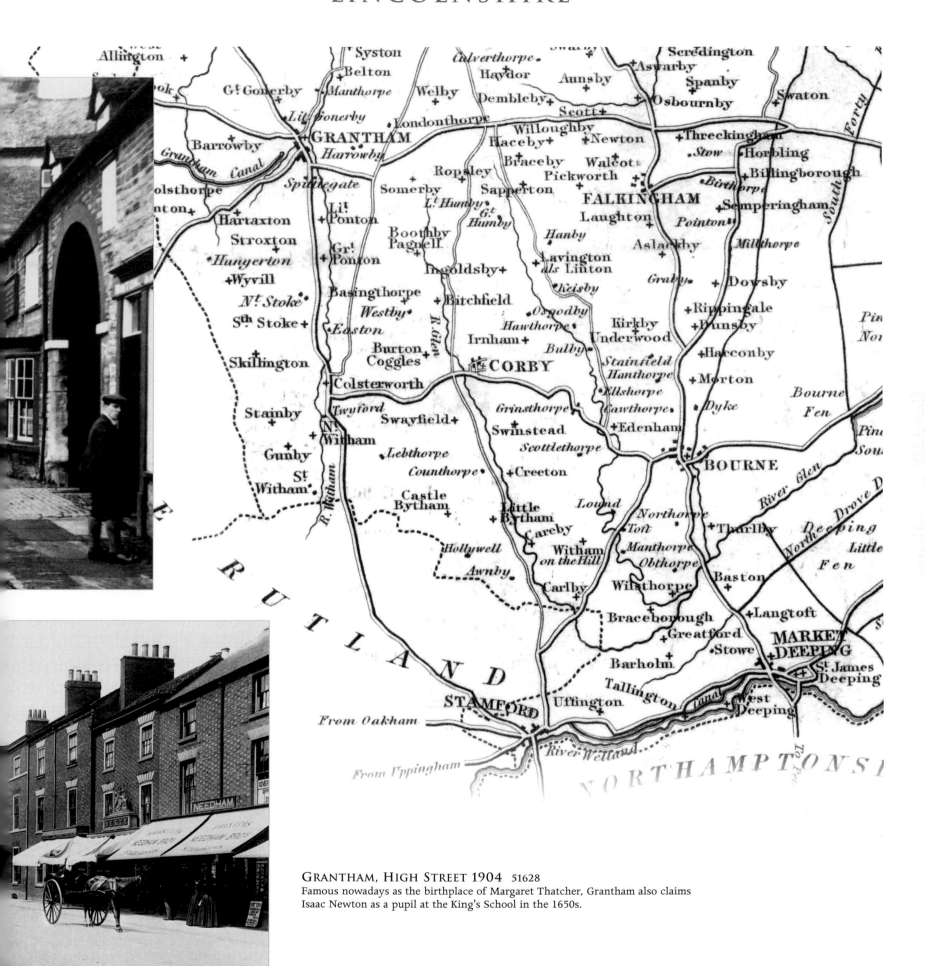

GRANTHAM, HIGH STREET 1904 51628
Famous nowadays as the birthplace of Margaret Thatcher, Grantham also claims
Isaac Newton as a pupil at the King's School in the 1650s.

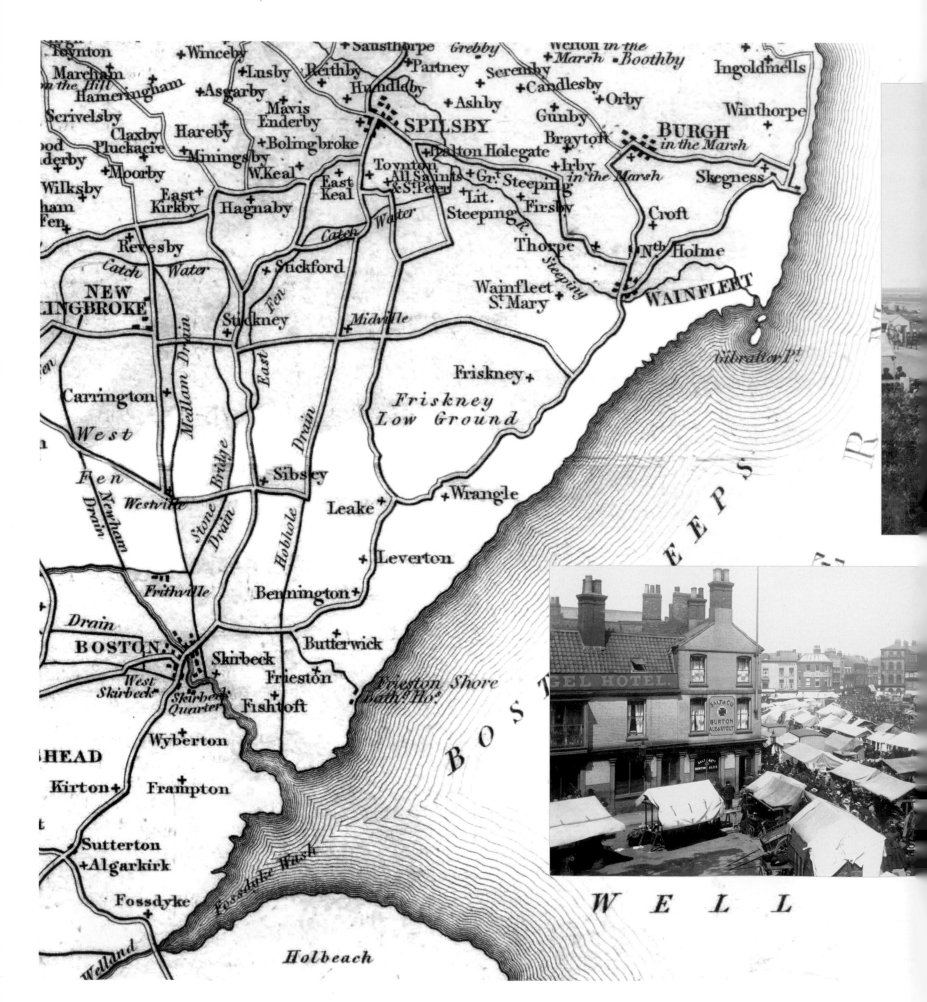

SKEGNESS, THE FIGURE EIGHT 1910 62862
The resort of Skegness was very much developed with day trips and excursions in mind, with influxes of visitors from the Midlands, especially Nottingham.

SKEGNESS, FROM THE PIER 1910 62843
Originally little more than a fishing village, Skegness was laid out from 1876 by the Earl of Scarborough, and acquired a pier in 1881.

BOSTON, MARKET PLACE 1899 43296
By the late 13th century the port of Boston was paying more customs dues than London, so successful was its wool trade.

rutland

Rutland's motto means 'much in little', which is very apt. England's smallest county has a wealth of countryside and unspoilt visitor attractions, including Rutland Water, the largest man-made lake in lowland England. The nearby Eyebrook Reservoir was the site of 'dummy runs' for the 'dambusters' raids during the Second World War. The castle of Oakham, Rutland's county town, has a tradition of receiving horseshoes from members of the Royal Family and peers of the realm: the earliest is said to have been given by Elizabeth I.

RUTLAND

UPPINGHAM, THE SCHOOL 1927 80317
During the medieval period, grammar schools were founded for the education of scholars across the class spectrum, but by the 19th century the so-called Great Schools had arrived in Engand. Founded in 1584 by Archdeacon Johnson in a single-roomed building, the Uppingham School expanded vastly during the last century.

UPPINGHAM, MARKET PLACE AND CHURCH 1932 85156
Uppingham has had an extremely active market since the 13th century. The grand church of St Peter and St Paul is from the 14th century, but was questionably 'restored' in 1842.

OAKHAM, THE CHURCH 1927 80295
Oakham's All Saints' Church is an elegant creation of c1300, with a tall, slim five-bay arcade and clerestory creating a tremendous feeling of space. Oakham was the home of Jeffrey Hudson, the world's smallest man, who hopped out of a pie to amaze Queen Henrietta Maria, wife of Charles II, in 1628. The delighted Queen appointed Jeffrey a page, even though he was only 18 inches high, and nine years old at the time. He died in 1682.

nottinghamshire

Nottinghamshire assumed much of its present character in th 18th century, when Enclosure Acts divided up the open fields of the villages into neat hawthorn-hedged small fields, and industry arrived, particularly around Nottingham itself, which began to grow quickly. Cotton mills and machine-lace factories supplanted the home-workers' hand-looms, stocking-frames and lace bobbins. The mechanisation of industry and deep coal-mining transformed parts of the county; within recent memory coal mines functioned all along the west of the county, and huge coal-fired power stations were built along the River Trent, supplied by barge and railway. Gresley's great steam locomotives hauled the Flying Scotsman and other expresses along the east coast main line of the London and North Eastern Region, passing through Newark and Retford on their way to Doncaster and the north.

NOTTINGHAM, CHEAPSIDE 1890 22823

The canal arrived at Nottingham in the 1790s, and the population shot up from about 11,000 in 1750 to 60,000 in 1850. The railway arrived in 1839 and 1852, and the town continued to expand. The Lace Market area prospered until the 1920s.

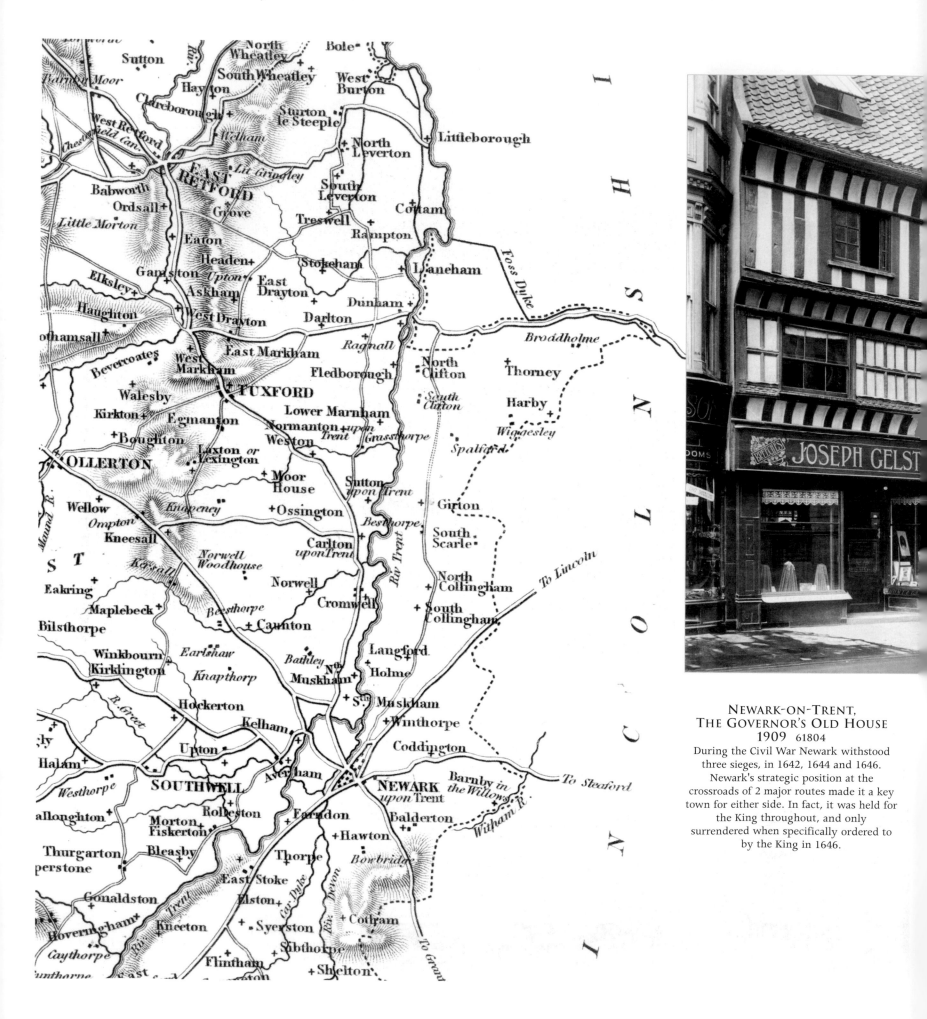

**NEWARK-ON-TRENT,
THE GOVERNOR'S OLD HOUSE
1909 61804**
During the Civil War Newark withstood
three sieges, in 1642, 1644 and 1646.
Newark's strategic position at the
crossroads of 2 major routes made it a key
town for either side. In fact, it was held for
the King throughout, and only
surrendered when specifically ordered to
by the King in 1646.

EAST RETFORD, MARKET SQUARE 1944
R261001
Retford was granted its charter in 1246 and its market place dates from soon after, although the town really prospered when the Great North Road was diverted through it in 1766, which turned it into a coaching town.

NEWARK-ON-TRENT, MARKET PLACE 1904
51736
In Georgian times Newark thrived as a coaching stop on the Great North Road; this, together with local trade and industrial growth, led to a great deal of rebuilding and re-fronting, which gives the town its present predominately Georgian character.

SOUTHWELL, KING STREET 1920 69472
This small, delightful town is dominated by its superb minster church. Founded by the Archbishop of York before AD956 as a minster church for the area with its own body or college of priests (prebendaries), the archbishops had a palace here until the mid 17th century.

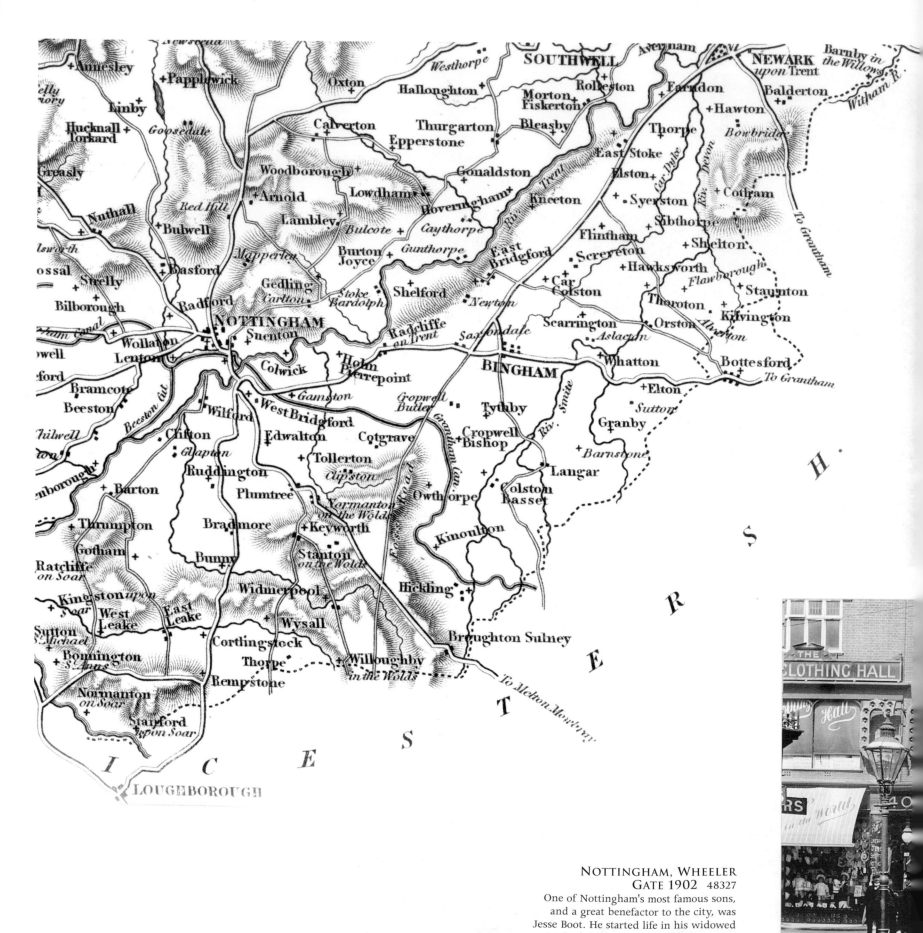

NOTTINGHAM, WHEELER
GATE 1902 48327
One of Nottingham's most famous sons,
and a great benefactor to the city, was
Jesse Boot. He started life in his widowed
mother's herbalist shop and went on to
found the Boot's Pure Drug Company in
1888. One of the earliest Boot's chemist
shops was in Pelham Street.

NOTTINGHAM, LONG ROW 1902
48326
The flamboyant hotel in the middle
distance was built in 1887 by the
somewhat quirky Nottingham architect
Watson Fothergill. Its lease expired in
1969 and its weirdly over-the-top
architecture was swept away, to be
replaced by a Littlewoods store.

derbyshire

Daniel Defoe, in his 'Tour Through Great Britain' (1724) roundly condemned
Derbyshire as 'the most desolate, wild and abandoned country in all England'.
However, tastes change; Derbyshire today is perhaps best known for the Peak
District National Park, covering 555 square miles of the north of the country.
Over 22 million days of visits are made to the National Park every year.

DERBY, THE TOWN HALL 1896 37776A
The Romans occupied the area now known as Little Derby. The town was later one of the 5 towns of the Danelaw, along with Lincoln, Leicester, Stamford and Nottingham. It fell to the Saxons in AD941. In 1745 Derby was the southernmost point reached by 'Bonnie Prince' Charles Edward Stuart during his invasion of England. Had he not turned back for Scotland, and eventual defeat at Culloden, the whole course of British history might have been different.

CHESTERFIELD, HIGH STREET 1896 37801
Chesterfield is famous for the crooked spire of St Mary and All Saints' Church. The lead-covered timber spire leans out of true some 6 feet to the south and over 4 feet to the west.

DERBY, IRONGATE AND ALL SAINTS' CHURCH 1896 37780
Rolls Royce engines and Crown Derby porcelain are just two famous products of Derby, which was created a city by Queen Elizabeth II during her Silver Jubilee in 1977.

MATLOCK BATH, DERWENT TERRACE 1892 31279
Although originally a lead-mining town, the warm springs at Matlock Bath began to attract public attention as early as 1698. After the 1850s the area began to rival Buxton as a spa resort.

staffordshire

Despite the lack of roads and navigable rivers in earlier times, the land-locked county of Staffordshire developed a variety of industries, excelling in pottery, iron and coal production. Pottery was being manufactured in and around Stafford from the 10th century. Though there was an abundant supply of coal for the pottery industry, local supplies of clay were insufficient to meet the growing demand, and potters were forced to import their clay from Devon and Cornwall. Josiah Wedgewood (1730 - 1795) was one of the prime movers for the building of the Trent and Mersey Canal, which opened in 1777. The Canal offered pottery manufacturers an economy of scale that could not be matched by the packhorse trains. The importance of the Canal in stimulating the pottery industry cannot be underestimated: its connections with no less than eight other canal systems, or significant branches, meant that most of England, and also overseas markets, could be supplied with its wares. In the iron industry, by the late 13th centuries forges were established at Cannock, Rugely and Sedgeley. These early forges smelted iron ore in a bloomery, which was often little more than an open hearth fired by charcoal. By Tudor times, the first blast furnaces were being introduced; the blast was provided by water-powered bellows. Water wheels also provided the motive power for the early drop hammers and the first slitting mills, which cut iron rods into workable lengths for nail makers. The use of coke in the early 18th century led to more than fifty coke-fired blast furnaces operating in the county by the end of the Napoleonic Wars. Staffordshire was also rich in coal. By the mid 17th century mining operations in south Staffordshire were producing an estimated annual turnover of 50,000 tonnes; this was to rise dramatically once the county was linked to the canal network. The north Staffordshire coalfield would prove to be the most productive, and was noted for its deep pits; many were well over 1,000 feet deep, and Stafford Colliery, Fenton, was the deepest in the country at over 3,300ft. Another great Staffordshire industry was brewing, centred on Burton upon Trent, a tradition said to have begun in the 13th century when one of the abbots of Burton Abbey discovered the local water was ideal for making good quality ale. Apparently Mary, Queen of Scots developed a taste for the ale during her stay at Tutbury Castle.

STAFFORD, THE ANCIENT HIGH HOUSE 1948 S411010
Stafford's oldest house is the four-storey, half-timbered High House, which dates from around 1555. It was here that King Charles I and Prince Rupert had their quarters during the King's march from Derby to Shrewsbury in September 1642, during the Civil War.

STONE, HIGH STREET 1900 46172
Stone grew up astride what was the most important road in medieval England, that between London and Chester, at that time a principal port for Ireland. In 1811 the population was around 6,000 people.

NEWCASTLE UNDER LYME, HIGH STREET 1965 N93049
During the first half of the 17th century Newcastle's clay pipe makers gained a reputation for turning out quality pipes, made from the clays between Shelton and Hanley Green, which were particularly suitable.

ECCLESHALL, HIGH STREET 1900 46156
The main road from London to Chester and Holyhead ran through Eccleshall. When the coaching trade developed around 1800, the town became an important stopping place. The coming of the railways, which linked Stafford to Birmingham by 1837, resulted in the collapse of this trade. Eccleshall was bypassed by both the canals and the railways, and its failure to develop after this has helped preserve its handsome main street.

STAFFORDSHIRE

LEEK, MARKET PLACE c1955 L379003
The town name of Leek is derived from 'Llech', meaning stone.
It stands at the southern edge of some of the most spectacular scenery in
the Midlands. This area has been attracting tourists for nearly 200 years,
but particularly since the 1840s, when the North Staffordshire Railway
opened its line through the Churnet Valley.

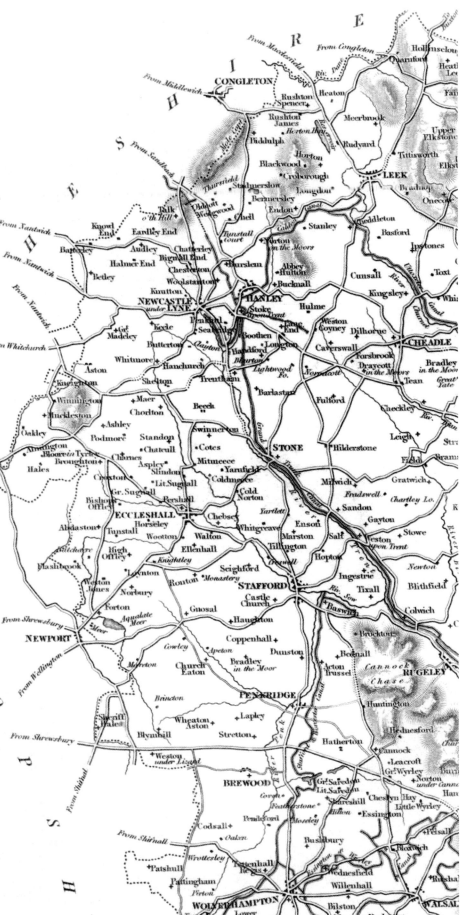

ECCLESHALL, HIGH STREET 1900 46158
The Royal Oak on Eccleshall's High Street became one of the town's two
main coaching inns, and had extensive stabling.

shropshire

Shropshire sits on the Marches (or borders) with Wales, and the land here has been fought over from the Dark Ages. King Offa in the late 8th century built his famous dyke through here to try and draw a line of demarcation between the English and the Welsh. During the Middle Ages the wool trade was of vital importance to the county's economy. Wool from all over northern and central Wales, as well as from the hills of Shropshire, came into the county's towns, was bought by the merchants and shipped down the Severn to Bristol and on to Europe. Evidence of the wealth of the merchants is to be seen all over the county, in buildings such as Stokesay Castle and many magnificent timbered town houses, particularly in Shrewsbury. In the 18th century Abraham Darby I mastered the technique of smelting iron using coke, instead of charcoal, and Shropshire was at the heart of technological development for the next one hundred years. The greatest innovators of the time came to Shropshire to see what was being done - people like Richard Trevithic, who invented the first steam locomotive, 'Ironmad' John Wilkinson, and Thomas Telford, the road and bridge builder. The jewel in Shropshire's crown was the famous iron bridge, opened in 1781, which is now the centre-point of the Ironbridge Gorge Museum. The first bridge in the world to be made of iron, the structure revolutionised bridge building and was the forerunner of modern steel-framed buildings.

NEWPORT, HIGH STREET
1893 41982
Charles Dickens visited Newport, where he heard the story of a local recluse, Elizabeth Parker, who had been jilted on her wedding day; this may have been the inspiration for Miss Havisham in 'Great Expectations'.

SHREWSBURY, WYLIE COP 1896 38099A

Shrewsbury has many fine medieval houses, where the flamboyant use of timber and elaborate carving showed off the wealth of the wool merchants who had them built.

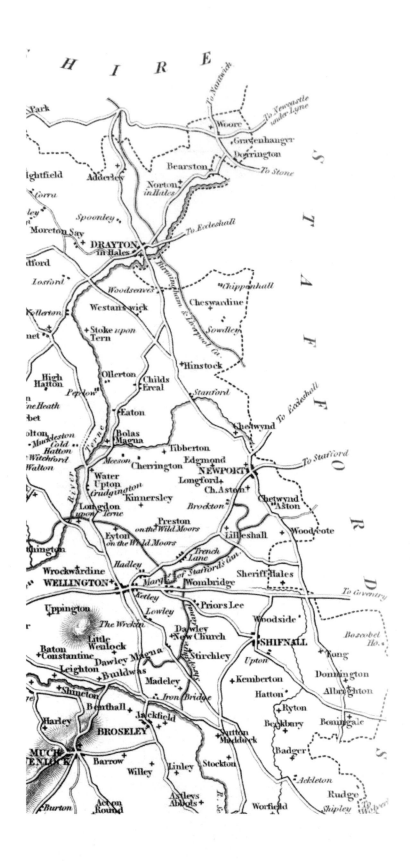

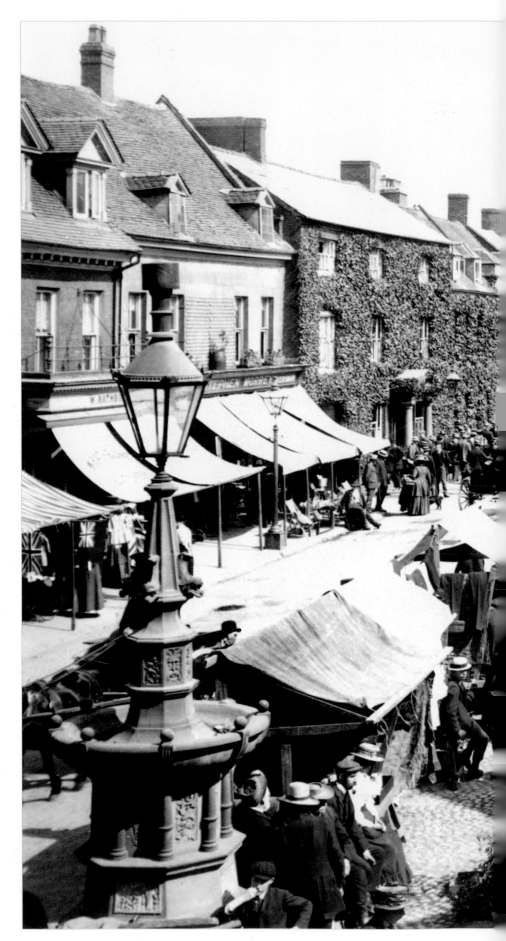

MARKET DRAYTON, MARKET DAY 63338
Market Drayton once had a court of 'pied poudre':here litigants could
settle their differences immediately they reached market - in other words,
while they still had dusty (or powdered) feet.

SHREWSBURY, THE RAVEN HOTEL AND CASTLE STREET 1911 63223
Shrewsbury is almost completely surrounded by the River Severn, so that most visitors to the town enter it over one of its bridges.

MUCH WENLOCK, GASKELL ARMS 1911 63261
The American author Henry James visited here in 1877. He describes Much Wenlock as an 'ancient little town...with no great din of vehicles... a dozen 'publics' (pubs), with tidy whitewashed cottages...and little girls bobbing curtsies in the street'.

LUDLOW, CORVE STREET 1910 62477
In Tudor times Ludlow was the administrative centre for Wales, and rivalled Shrewsbury in importance.

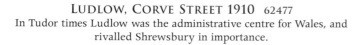

BRIDGNORTH, NORTH GATE 1896 38127
In medieval times Bridgnorth was the second most important town in Shropshire, owing to its position on the junction of two trade routes - river traffic to north and south, and road traffic to east and west.

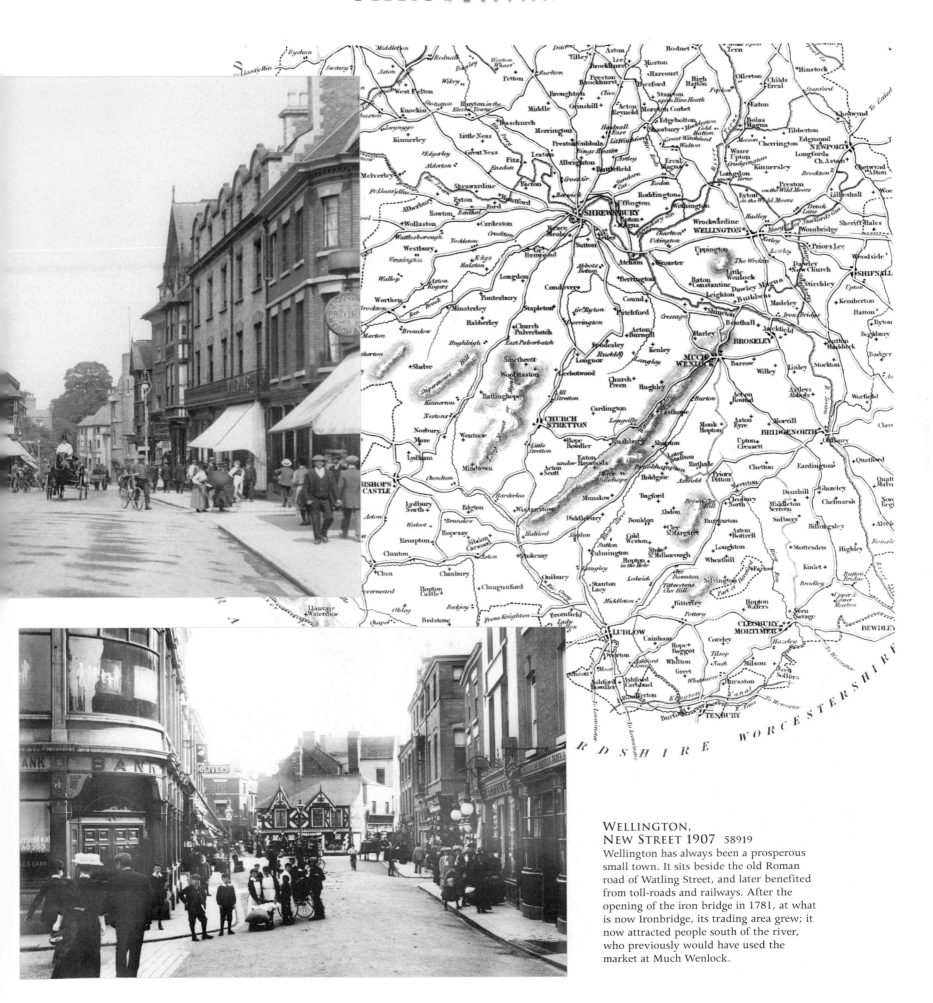

WELLINGTON, NEW STREET 1907 58919

Wellington has always been a prosperous small town. It sits beside the old Roman road of Watling Street, and later benefited from toll-roads and railways. After the opening of the iron bridge in 1781, at what is now Ironbridge, its trading area grew; it now attracted people south of the river, who previously would have used the market at Much Wenlock.

cheshire

Situated on the west coast of England in what is sometimes referred to as northern England and sometimes central England, Cheshire is a county of delightful contrasts. These range from the silted marshlands of the Wirral, to the undulating agricultural country of the south of the county with its many black and white timber houses, and on eastwards to the hill country along the edges of the Peaks, from the historic home of ancient British legions at Chester to the industrial heartlands along the Mersey valley. One industry has been of major importance to Cheshire since the Roman times - the salt industry, based in the centre of the county in the towns of Northwich, Middlewich and Nantwich ('wich' in Old English meant salt works). However, salt was not the only product being transported around Cheshire and beyond. From the Middle Ages Chester had been a major centre through which wool and cloth were exported. By the 17th century other goods were passing through the county - fragile china from the Potteries, iron products from the new industrial centres of Shropshire and the Black Country, and coal and other raw materials being brought to the manufactories. Many of these goods were moved along rivers, but the rivers were often impassable owing to floods or drought. To begin with, work was done to make them navigable. One of the earliest rivers to be cut in this way was the River Weaver, forming what is now known as the Weaver Navigation. Then, in 1759, the Duke of Bridgewater financed the building of the first proper canal - the Bridgewater Canal. When the first stretch of this canal opened in 1761 it revolutionised the transportation of goods, and ushered in a frenzy of canal building projects all around the country.

RUNCORN, THE TRANSPORTER BRIDGE c1906 43432A
The transporter bridge between Widnes and Runcorn was opened in 1905, but was re-opened in 1913 after being strengthened, and with a new electric motor added. Widnes Corporation maintained and paid for the bridge until it closed down in 1961.

CHESTER, THE CROSS 1903 49881

Around AD79, the Romans established a fort at a site they called Deva, because it was the lowest crossing point over the River Dee. The legionary fortress covered an area of around 60 acres, and its layout has served as the ground plan for the city of Chester ever since. In Roman times several roads met at the site now known as The Cross, and later a medieval cross stood nearby, until it was demolished during the Civil War. The cross was restored to its original site in 1975.

CHESTER, EASTGATE 1903 49887
The Eastgate, which was the entry point of the Roman road, the Via Devana, was rebuilt as an elegant arch in 1769. The clock standing on top of the Eastgate was presented to the city by Edward Evans-Lloyd in 1897 to commemorate Queen Victoria's Diamond Jubilee.

ECCLESTON, THE FERRY 1895 36455
The flat-bottomed ferry across the Dee at Eccleston (fare 1d) was attached to both sides of the river and winched across. The ferry would have been capable of transporting horses, carts, wagons and coaches.

HALE, MAIN STREET 1907 58620
This photograph shows a typical example of a suburban post office in the Edwardian era. Housed in Kennerley's drapery store, local mail would be sorted and delivered from here. There was even a delivery on Christmas day.

NANTWICH, HIGH STREET 1898 42179
Cattle drovers from Wales would have entered Nantwich along Welsh Row in order to trade their animals for salt in Nantwich's market. A town of major importance in Cheshire's salt industry, most of Nantwich's old buildings were destroyed in a severe fire during the reign of Queen Elizabeth I.

ALTRINCHAM, STAMFORD NEW ROAD 1907 58622
The quiet market town of Altrincham on the edge of the Cheshire Plain became a cotton-weaving centre linked to Manchester in the Industrial Revolution of the 19th century. In the early 20th century Altrincham's Unicorn Hotel was AA recommended, a fourteen-bed establishment with garaging for two automobiles.

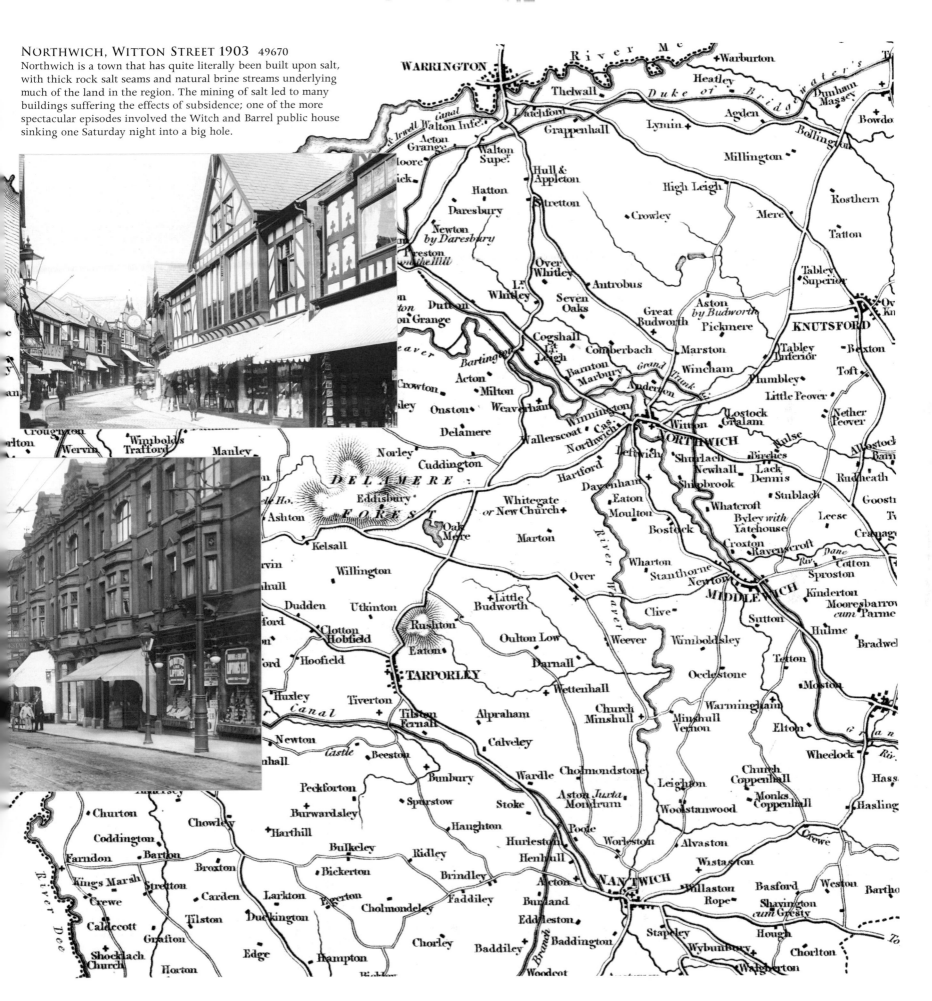

NORTHWICH, WITTON STREET 1903 49670

Northwich is a town that has quite literally been built upon salt, with thick rock salt seams and natural brine streams underlying much of the land in the region. The mining of salt led to many buildings suffering the effects of subsidence; one of the more spectacular episodes involved the Witch and Barrel public house sinking one Saturday night into a big hole.

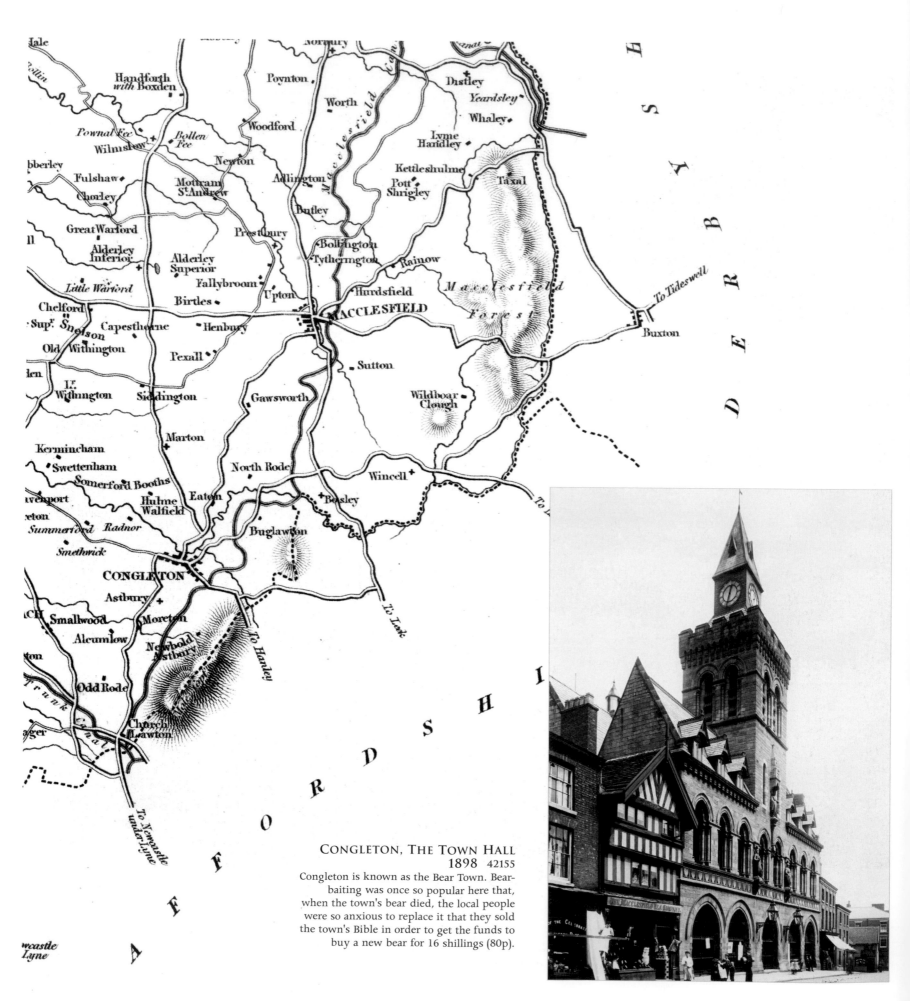

CONGLETON, THE TOWN HALL
1898 42155
Congleton is known as the Bear Town. Bear-
baiting was once so popular here that,
when the town's bear died, the local people
were so anxious to replace it that they sold
the town's Bible in order to get the funds to
buy a new bear for 16 shillings (80p).

CHESHIRE

WILMSLOW, GROVE STREET 1897 39604
Like many other towns around Manchester, Wilmslow grew enormously in the 18th century with the development of industries linked to local silk and cotton mills. Quarry Bank cotton mill near Wilmslow was established in 1784. It is now open to the public, where it is possible to see the accommodation for the apprentice children who once worked there under the most appalling conditions.

MACCLESFIELD, MARKET PLACE 1898 42599
Macclesfield's wealth was founded on its silk industry; there was a mill here as early as 1743. One of the mills, Paradise Mill, which was working until 1981, survives today as a museum dedicated to the industry.

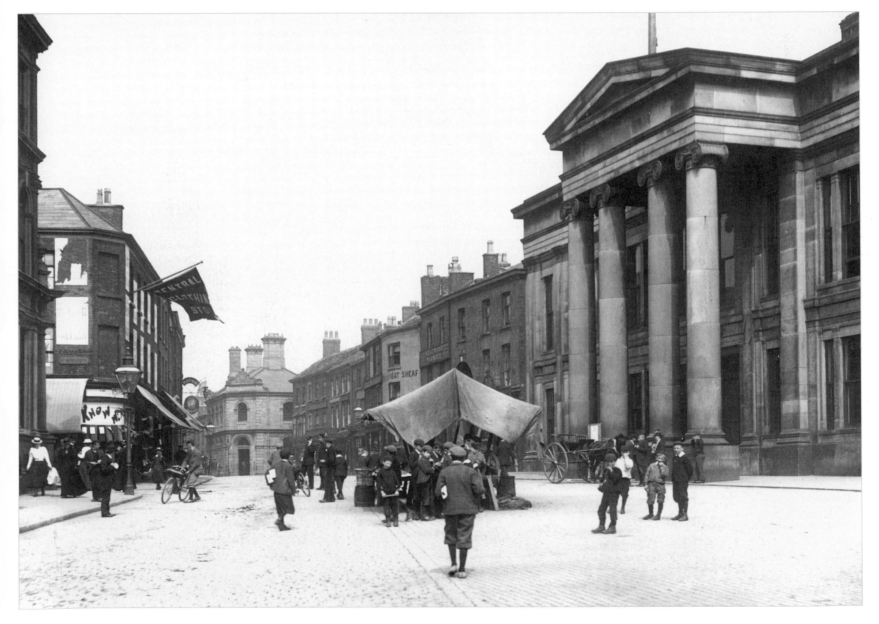

lancashire

Described in a 1930s guidebook to England as one of the richest counties in the land, Lancashire was then, and still is, rightly deserving of such praise. The region's richness extends far beyond the industrial and commercial wealth that the author of the time had in mind, for Lancashire's borders encompass a surprising diversity and interest in its cities, towns, villages and countryside that few other regions equal. True, the south and east can hardly be described as 'pretty', but the towns, which were the birthplace of the Industrial Revolution, have other qualities that make them worthy of investigation. The profits generated by their factories and mills were vast, and the investments in civic and commercial building that followed produced some of the 18th and 19th centuries' most eloquent architectural statements. Those same towns were also cradles of cultural development, for in them were established many fine public museums and art galleries, and in Manchester the German-born musician Sir Charles Hallé founded one of the country's finest orchestras in 1848. In dramatic contrast, Lancashire's wild countryside can sometimes seem as remote as anywhere:
a person can roam all day across the moors, hardly meeting another along the way.

LANCASTER
THE TOWN HALL 1912
64215
This photograph shows Dalton Square, the Town Hall, and the Queen Victoria monument. It was in Dalton Square, named after the Dalton family, that cattle and livestock markets were held when Market Square had proved too small. Lancaster Council had always intended to move its town hall here, and had already purchased the land for this purpose about 15 years before the new town hall opened.

MANCHESTER, MARKET STREET c1885 18266
Originally a narrow street of shops, houses and workshops, the redevelopment and widening of Market Street took place between 1822 and 1834 at a cost in excess of £250,000. Our picture was taken about 1885, when the Palmer Oil Company had their Manchester office above J S Moss & Son, and the Manchester Advance & Discount Bank could be found at number 39. In the distance is a parcel delivery van operated by 'Parcelhorse' - not Parcelforce.

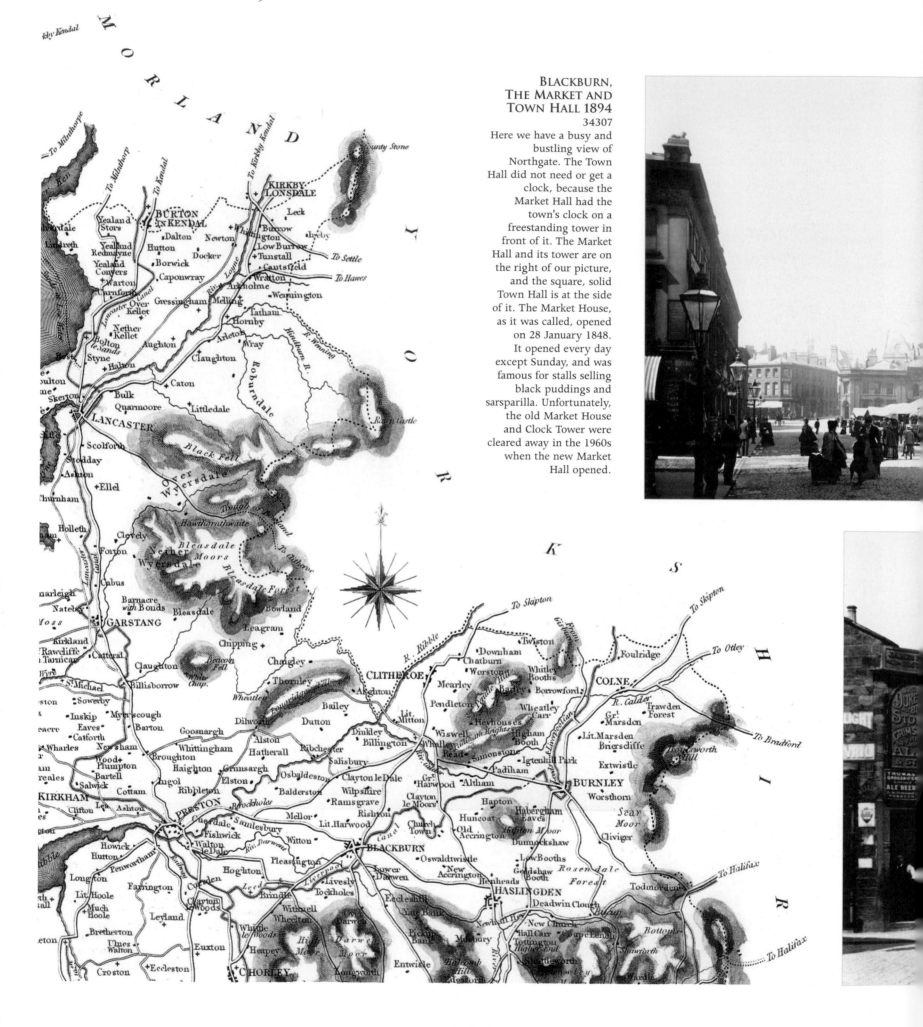

BLACKBURN, THE MARKET AND TOWN HALL 1894
34307
Here we have a busy and bustling view of Northgate. The Town Hall did not need or get a clock, because the Market Hall had the town's clock on a freestanding tower in front of it. The Market Hall and its tower are on the right of our picture, and the square, solid Town Hall is at the side of it. The Market House, as it was called, opened on 28 January 1848. It opened every day except Sunday, and was famous for stalls selling black puddings and sarsparilla. Unfortunately, the old Market House and Clock Tower were cleared away in the 1960s when the new Market Hall opened.

CLITHEROE
BRUNGERLEY BRIDGE 1894 34346
The River Ribble in summer is the most pleasant of rivers, and to picnic and paddle by its banks has been a delight for many centuries. Here we see a photograph of children enjoying a day at Brungerley Bridge, a popular venue for relaxation at Bank Holidays. Waddow Hall, at the north side of the bridge, is a 16th-century building with additions of 1630. It was the home of the dowager lady of the Tempest family, and was bought by the Girl Guide Association in 1928.

BURNLEY, DUKE BAR 1906 54183
Duke Bar is on the outskirts of Burnley. The Duke of York public house can be seen in the centre of our picture. Burnley was one of the few towns where steam trams were employed after the horse buses and before the electric trams that the corporation introduced in the early 1900s. Note the wonderfully lettered sign for the Duke Bar Bottle Stores on the left of the picture, which promotes 'Grimshaw's Lancastrian Ales & Stout'. The railway arrived in Burnley from Accrington in September 1848, and six months later the line went on to Colne. The railway had a large impact on the town, especially as there was so much coal mining in the area.

WARRINGTON, CHURCH STREET 1894
33805
Sitting beside the River Mersey, Warrington developed as an important junction for both road and rail traffic. At the time of this photograph the annual event known as Walking Day was still practiced. Every year, children from the town's churches, chapels and Sunday Schools dressed in white and paraded through the streets. The custom survived until recent times. Warrington became part of Cheshire after the county boundaries were changed in 1974.

PRESTON, FISHERGATE 1903 50065
The tower with its clock belongs to the Preston Baptist Church; the Town Hall spire can be seen further up Fishergate. There is an interesting diversity of shops, from a plumber's to the Cocoa Rooms - this has always been Preston's main shopping street.

LANCASTER, CHURCH STREET 1896
37381
This view is looking up Church Street towards St Mary's Parish Church and the Priory. The printing office of the Lancaster Guardian was the second building on the right. Church Street was used as an open market on Lancaster Fair days. As the town was important, its charter allowed 4 of these Fair days - 3 April, 1 May, 5 July and 10 October, which was also the Winter Fair and Hiring Day. Lancaster's first charter of 1199 gave Wednesday and Saturday as market days.

LIVERPOOL,
THE QUADRANT 1890 26662

This photograph shows Lime Street Station and the London and North Western Railway Hotel. Lime Street was the main station for London & North Western services to London, Manchester, Edinburgh and Glasgow. The hotel was at the top end of the price scale, along with the Adelphi and the Lancashire & Yorkshire Hotel at Exchange Station. In 1906, rooms at these hotels started from 4s 6d a night; dinner from 5s.

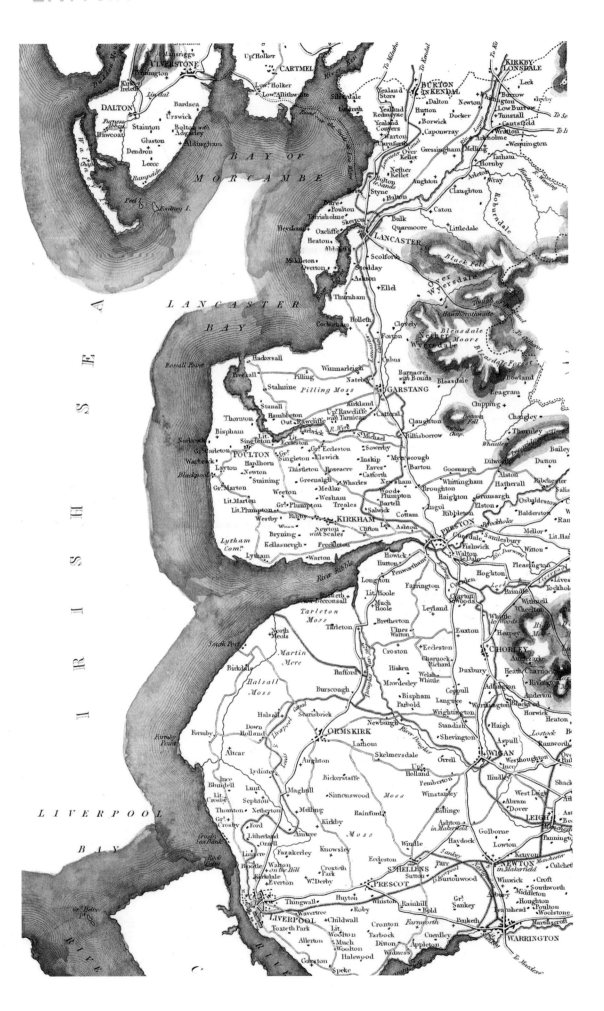

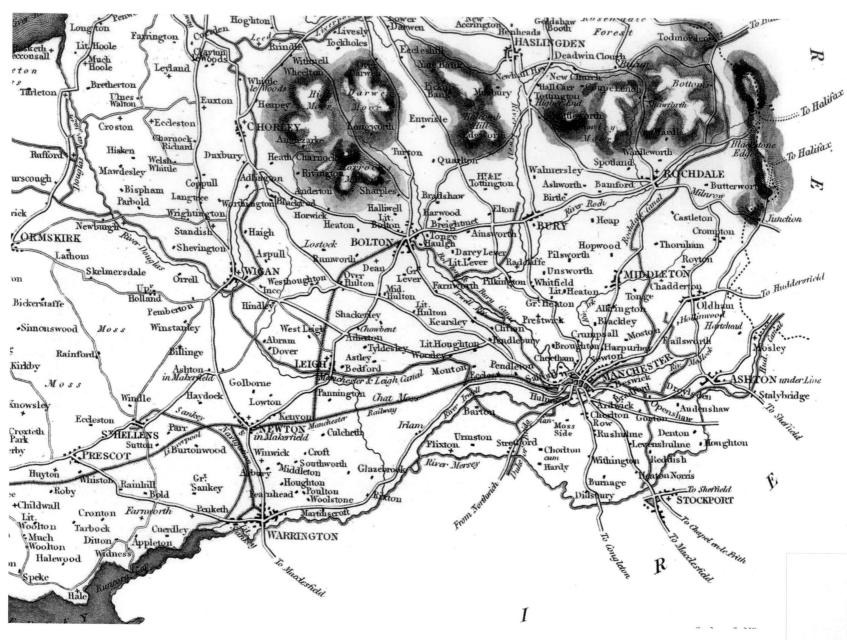

MANCHESTER, ST ANN'S SQUARE 1885 18263
This view looks towards the Royal Exchange and St Mary's Gate. This was one of the principle cab ranks in Manchester, and licensing, fares and conditions were regulated by the local authority. Cabs could be hired by time at 2s 6d per hour, or by distance, the fare dependent upon the number of people sharing.

MANCHESTER, PICCADILLY 1887 22159

This photograph was taken from the Queen's Hotel and looking across Piccadilly towards Market Street, where we can see Lewis' Department Store. In the foreground is a poster advertising the Royal Jubilee Exhibition, which was opened by the Prince of Wales and ran from May to October 1887.

ROCHDALE, CHURCH STEPS 1913 65603

This flight of 122 steps leads up to the parish church dedicated to St Chad. A local legend says that the church was to have been built on the banks of the River Roch, but every night the materials were mysteriously shifted to the top of a nearby hill by 'goblin builders'.

MANCHESTER, THE ROYAL JUBILEE EXHIBITION, ROYAL ENTRANCE 1887 21901

The idea that the celebration of Queen Victoria's Jubilee should include an exhibition featuring Manchester's business, commerce and industry was first discussed in 1886. A 32-acre site adjoining the Botanical Gardens at Old Trafford was chosen, as it had both rail and tramway connections. Note the mock-up of the cathedral tower.

yorkshire

Yorkshire's history encompasses the past lives of monks in the monasteries, the sheep farmers high up on the Dales, affluent gentry in their Victorian houses, fisher-folk along the dramatic coastline, workers in the teeming new cities, and coal miners working the rich seams of South Yorkshire to fuel the county's steel mills. The middle part of Yorkshire, the West Riding, originally extended down to Sheffield and was the powerhouse for the industrialisation of manufacturing. Bradford and Leeds grasped the opportunities to trade in wool. A ready supply of sheep in the upper dales, and an ingenuity for inventing looms and spinning machines, meant that the West Riding was at the forefront of the global trade in textiles. The wealth that was created was invested in splendid civic buildings in the area, and eventually transformed the stinking slums into the vibrant towns and cities of today. The northern Dales contain the National Park; Victorian authors and artists came here to seek inspiration, but the area was also important for lead mining, smelt mills and stone quarrying. Along Yorkshire's coast are quaint villages and Victorian spas. Scarborough was the first town where the commercial possibilities of a seaside holiday were exploited, although in the early days it attracted the gentry for health reasons, rather than pleasure seekers from the urban West Riding. The whole coastline is dotted with villages clinging to the side of steep and constantly eroding cliffs, which attract visitors in search of picturesque views; King George III is said to have temporarily escaped from his mental madness after gazing at the vista from Ravenscar to Robin Hood's Bay.

YORK, CONEY STREET 1909 61723

The walled city of York was for centuries the second most important city in England. Fortified by the Romans, it was here in AD306 that Constantine the Great was proclaimed emperor. The Victorians loved York and, before the coming of the railway, travellers could get here either by stage or mail coach; there was also a steamboat service to and from London.

WHITBY, BAXTER GATE 1923 74309
In AD644 the system for dating Easter was fixed in a meeting between the Celtic and Roman Churches at
Whitby's abbey - the meeting was known as the Synod of Whitby.

BRADFORD, TYRREL STREET 1903 49713

Without doubt Bradford was the centre of the woollen and worsted industry, not only in this country but also throughout the world. The Victorian traveller would have found the city skyline a veritable forest of mill chimneys, but there were other industries. Bradford was on the western edge of the great Yorkshire coalfield, and because the coal was near the surface it could be mined relatively inexpensively. Also close by were the ironworks of Bowling and Low Moor.

HARROGATE, VALLEY GARDENS 1907 58645

Harrogate is one of the oldest and most loved of the English spa towns. The mineral springs were discovered in 1571 but the town was not developed as a spa until the 1840s. By 1906 it was being described as having a high and bracing situation among the Yorkshire moors, and ranks with Bath and Buxton among the three chief inland watering places of England.

HAWES 1908 60795

Granted a market charter by William III, Hawes later became a centre for textiles, quarrying and the production of Wensleydale cheese.

SETTLE, MARKET DAY 1921 71339

Settle lies on the road between Skipton and Ingleton. Trade in the town increased dramatically once the Keighley to Kendall turnpike road opened, making Settle a premier coaching route. The 72-mile Settle to Carlisle railway line, built between 1869-76, brought some of the first tourists to the Yorkshire Dales. The line had 325 bridges, 21 viaducts, 14 tunnels and 21 stations.

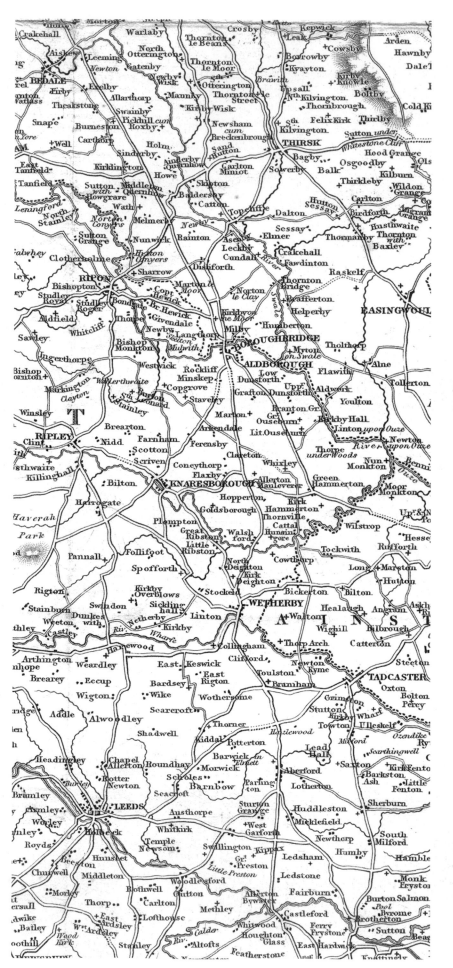

KNARESBOROUGH, MARKET DAY 1921 71687
Coaches used to arrive and depart from the inns and taverns along Knaresborough High Street. From the Bay Horse there was a coach to Selby; from the Elephant and Castle there was one to Thirsk, Leeds, York and Harrogate. From the Black Swan, a wagon ran every Monday, Wednesday and Friday to York.

Situated in a deep ravine on the estuary of the River Esk, Whitby once earned its living from the sea, either by whaling, fishing, coastal trading or shipbuilding. The coming of the railway put Whitby on the tourist map; its harbour-side streets, ruined abbey and souvenirs made from jet, which is a fossilized wood found locally, all proved a magnet for holiday-makers. The holiday trade encouraged much of the development of the town.

MIDDLESBROUGH, LINTHORPE ROAD 1913 66411

Middlesbrough's population saw a dramatic rise during the 1800s. In 1801 it consisted of just four houses and twenty-five people. Things changed however when Middlesbrough was chosen by the Stockton & Darlington Railway as the site for a number of staithes, where coal could be shipped for delivery by sea. Joseph Pease was responsible not only for extending the railway to Middlesbrough but also for laying out the new town, which consisted of a dozen or so streets of houses, a market square, town hall and a parish church. By 1841 the population had rocketed to 5,463 inhabitants; the staithes were moving around 1.5 million tons of coal a year, and additional industries had already sprung up in the form of a pottery, foundry and a rolling mill. An ironworks followed, and in less than a hundred years Middlesbrough had grown from an obscure hamlet to a large industrial town of 91,000 people.

SCARBOROUGH, SPA SALOON 1890 23450
Scarborough was a popular spa town on the Yorkshire coast. Its waters were discovered around 1626. As a spa town Scarborough attracted the wealthier visitor - objections were raised against the coming of the railway on the grounds that it was felt that the town wanted nothing to do with the lower social orders. The watering place had no wish for a greater influx of 'vagrants', and those who had no money to spend.

REDCAR, THE PIER 1896 37594
Though popular, Redcar suffered for years, along with other Teeside resorts, owing to the reluctance of the North Eastern Railway to operate Sunday services for fear of upsetting the church-goers.

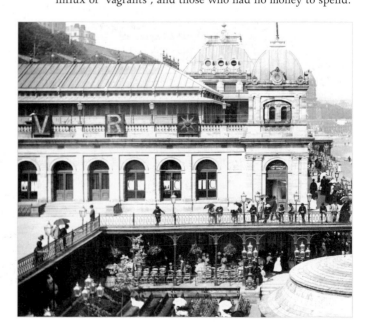

BOOTHAM BAR 1886
18443

This, the northern gate, stands on the site of the Roman Porta Principalis, the gateway of Eboracum. The barbican was demolished in 1835. The name Bootham derives from Buthum, 'at the booths'; this probably related to market stalls that were set up nearby. The medieval statues that can just be seen on top of the bar are in very poor condition and are hardly recognisable as figures.

SHEFFIELD, FITZALAN SQUARE 1902 48268
Famous since the 14th century for cutlery, it was Benjamin Huntsman's discovery that steel could be purified by using a crucible that led to Sheffield becoming the steel capital of Britain. Forges, metalworking shops and steelworks came in all shapes and sizes, from those employing just a handful of men to the industrial giants like Firth Brown and Hadfields. There were other industries, such as the Yorkshire Engine Co. which built railway locomotives, and there were several collieries within easy reach of the city centre.

YORK, THE STATION 1909 61850

For centuries the Ouse had been used to transport people and goods in and out of York. In the mid 1830s there was even a steamer service linking York with London. The journey took over 30 hours, and was an acceptable alternative to being shaken and bounced along the Great North Road in a mail coach. The coming of the railway put York firmly on the tourist map. Though the lines were owned by the North Eastern, no less than 5 other companies had running powers into the city.

westmoreland

The ancient counties of Cumberland and Westmoreland, and that part of Lancashire known as 'Lancashire-over-the-Sands' were amalgamated in the 1974 local government boundary changes of 1974 to become Cumbria. This area had been part of a British kingdom called Rheged in the Dark Ages at the end of the Roman administration, and was later incorporated into the Saxon kingdom of Northumbria, which extended on both sides of the Pennines. The name Westmoreland was first recorded in the Anglo-Saxon Chronicle in AD966, and simply means 'the land of the Westmoringas', or the people who lived to the west of the moors of Yorkshire. In 1810 William Wordsworth's 'Guide to the Lake District' was not only the first tourist guide to the area but also the first recorded suggestion that the area should be set aside as 'a sort of national property, in which every man has a right and interest who has an eye to perceive and a heart to enjoy'. In 1951 the Lake District became the largest of Britain's 11 National Parks, with 20 million visitors a year.

BOWNESS-ON-WINDERMERE, PLEASURE STEAMER 'TEAL' 1896
38795

The coming of the railway in 1847 increased the popularity of the Lake District as a health-giving resort for people from the industrial towns and cities of the north-west. In the small town of Bowness many hotels sprang up to accommodate these visitors, and pleasure steamers ran, taking their passengers from Bowness Pier on a pleasure trip to enjoy the scenery from the lake.

AMBLESIDE, MARKET PLACE 1912 64302
At the beginning of the 20th century, at the height of the tourist season, visitors could take a coach and horses tour
from Ambleside to Keswick and Windermere.

NEWBY BRIDGE 1914 67414
Newby Bridge takes its name from the five-arched bridge across the River Leven, originally built in the 16th century.

WINDERMERE, ABOVE WATERHEAD 1912 64319
Steamboats began to bring tourists up and down Lake Windermere from 1845. The landing at the mouth of the lake was not large enough, so a new pier was built at Waterhead, which soon became a tourist centre in its own right. The town of Windermere was originally known as Birthwaite, but its name was changed to match that of the nearby lake when the Kendal and Windermere Railway reached the town in 1847.

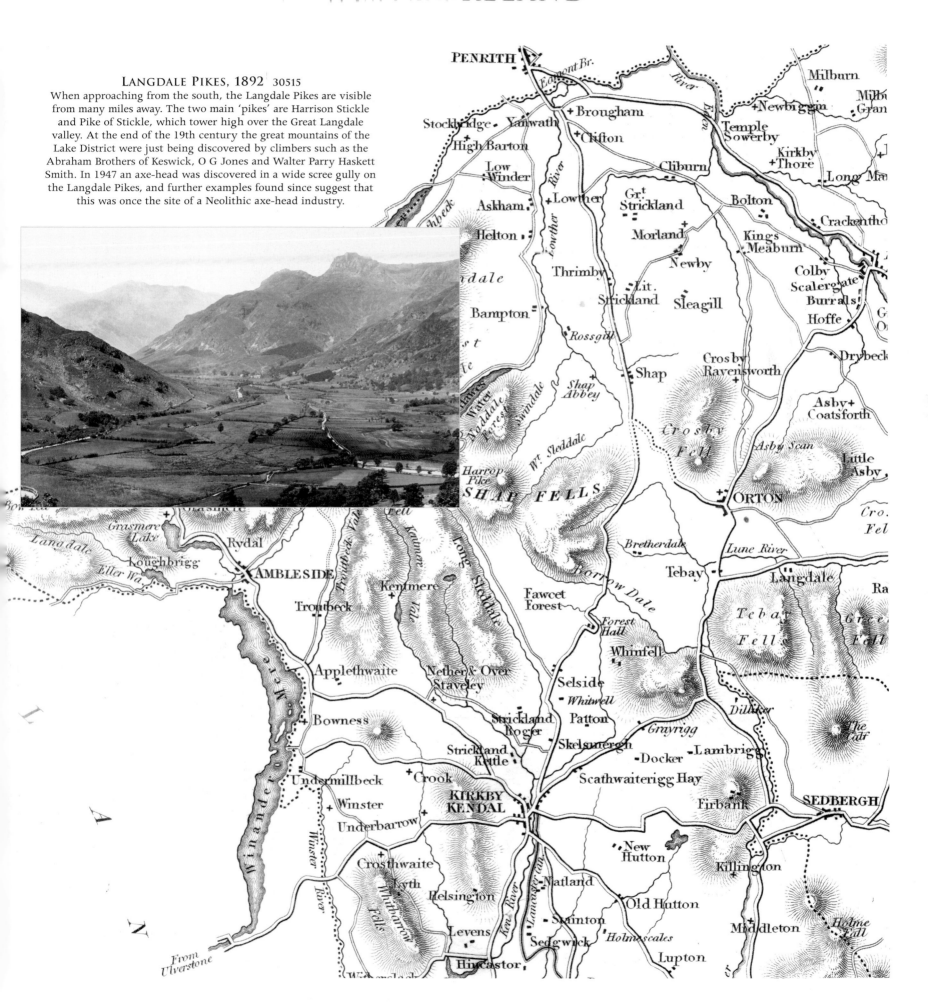

LANGDALE PIKES, 1892 30515

When approaching from the south, the Langdale Pikes are visible from many miles away. The two main 'pikes' are Harrison Stickle and Pike of Stickle, which tower high over the Great Langdale valley. At the end of the 19th century the great mountains of the Lake District were just being discovered by climbers such as the Abraham Brothers of Keswick, O G Jones and Walter Parry Haskett Smith. In 1947 an axe-head was discovered in a wide scree gully on the Langdale Pikes, and further examples found since suggest that this was once the site of a Neolithic axe-head industry.

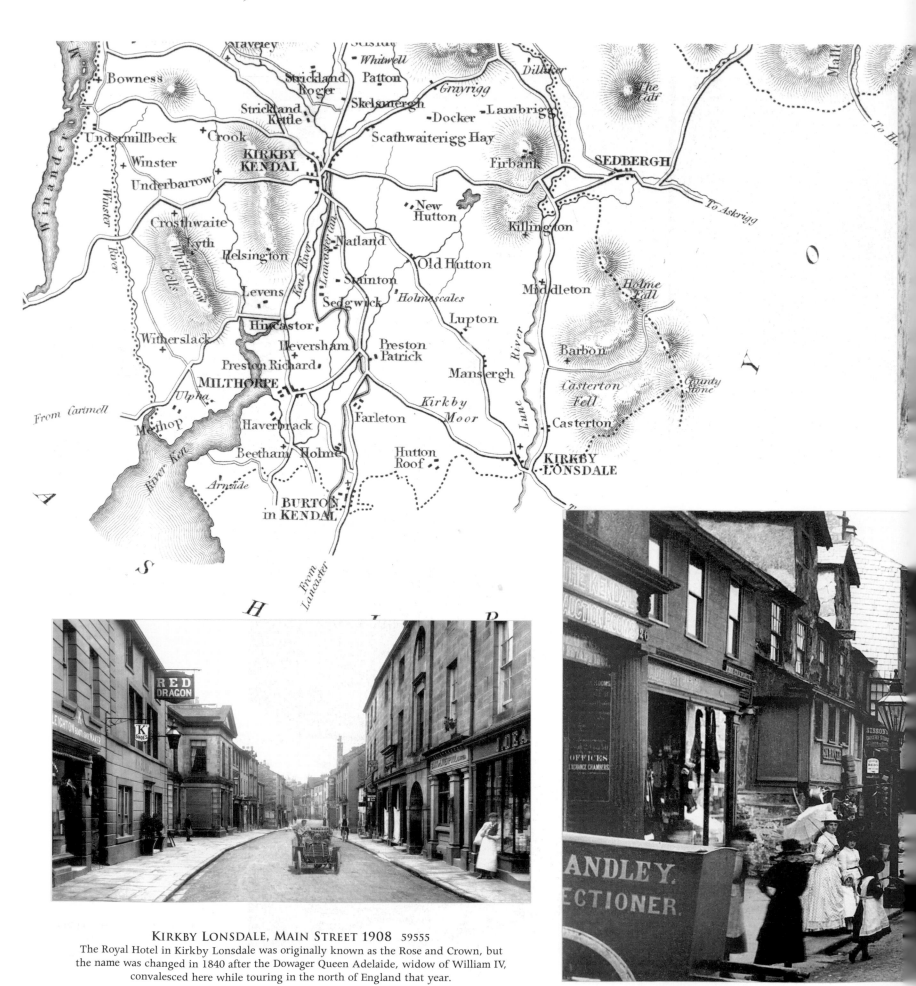

KIRKBY LONSDALE, MAIN STREET 1908 59555

The Royal Hotel in Kirkby Lonsdale was originally known as the Rose and Crown, but the name was changed in 1840 after the Dowager Queen Adelaide, widow of William IV, convalesced here while touring in the north of England that year.

KENDAL, AN OLD YARD OFF STRICKLANDGATE 1914 67398

Kendal, on the mouth of the River Kent, was founded on the wealth won from the wool of Lakeland sheep; its motto is 'Pannis mihi Panis', which means 'wool is my bread'. But wool was not Kendal's only industry, and many other trades were set up in the many yards which lead off the main street of this southern gateway to the lakes.

ARNSIDE, FROM THE BEACH 2894 34128

Once a thriving port and Westmoreland's only link to the sea, Arnside eventually lost its trade to better placed harbours.

KENDAL, STRICKLANDGATE 1888 21088

The name 'Stricklandgate' means 'the road leading to the stirk (cattle) land', and refers to the use of the road to drive cattle into market from the north.

cumberland

Cumberland is now part of the larger area known as Cumbria, but its name is ancient: it is a Celtic title meaning 'land of the Cumbrians' or Britons, and derives from the Welsh 'Cymry'; the name was recorded in the Anglo-Saxon Chronicle of AD945. Cumberland was originally part of the British kingdom of Strathclyde. This country on the border with Scotland has been fought over for centuries. The earliest tourists to the area were overwhelmed by the 'horrid' and 'frightful' nature of the mountains and crags; it was the influence of Wordworth and the other Romantic poets that promoted the idea of the fells having their own beauty and grandeur. There are 16 lakes in the Lake District, but only one, Bassenthwaite, is actually called a lake. All the rest are 'meres' or 'waters', while the smaller mountain lakes are known as 'tarns'; they were all formed in troughs gouged out by Ice Age glaciers.

GREYSTOKE, THE CHURCH 1893 32959
Greystoke Church dates from the 13th century. Its tower was used as a refuge by the villagers, who hid there from marauding Scots.

DERWENT WATER, FRIAR'S CRAG 1893 32862

Friar's Crag obtained its name as the embarkation point for monks crossing to St Herbert's Island. A single stone oblelisk on
the summit of Friar's Crag commemorates the great Victorian critic and Lake District conservationist John Ruskin.
Derwent Water, 3 miles long and 1 mile wide, is formed by a widening of the River Derwent.

durham

County Durham's borders once extended from the south bank of the Tyne to the north bank of the Tees; the western border extended into the Pennines, the north-western along the banks of the Derwent. It was a county of contrasts, with collieries, steelworks, quarries, shipyards and heavy industry as well as agriculture. In the 19th and early 20th centuries the north-east was an industrial powerhouse. As late as 1947, when the National Coal Board was formed, there were 127 active pits employing 108,000 mine workers. The shipyards along the Durham side of the Tyne, and along the Wear and the Tees, were at the forefront of world shipbuilding and repairs. The famous yard of Palmer Bros at Jarrow did not survive the Depression of the 1930s, but 650 years of shipbuilding at Sunderland only ended in 1989, when the North East Shipbuilders' Southwick yard was closed.

SUNDERLAND, FAWCETT STREET 1890 S263001
By the mid 19th century Sunderland had become the greatest shipbuilding centre in the world, as well as a major port for the export of coal brought down the river by barges.

DURHAM, FRAMWELLGATE BRIDGE 1892 30739

Durham has become a major tourist centre for visitors to the north of England; both its cathedral and castle are now designated as World Heritage Sites, on a par with Stonehenge and the Taj Mahal. Framwellgate was Durham's first bridge over the Wear; it was ordered to be built by Bishop Flambard in 1128, The peninsula end was originally defended by a gatehouse, but this fortification was demolished in 1760.

BISHOP AUCKLAND, NEWGATE STREET 1914   67136
By the 18th century Bishop Auckland was an important market town at a crossing point of the Wear. Its growth, however, owed much to the development of coal mining to the east and south-west.

DURHAM, OLD ELVET 1914   67127
Old Elvet was once the site of Durham's horse fair. The Royal County Hotel is noted for its balcony, on which prominent leaders of the Labour Party and mineworkers acknowledged the parades on Miner's Gala Day.

DARLINGTON, TUBWELL ROW 1903   50008
Darlington Railway Centre and Museum, in North Road Station, houses the Stockton and Darlington No 1 'Locomotion', designed and built by George Stephenson. She achieved a maximum speed of 15mph when she hauled the 34-wagon inaugural train on the world's first public passenger railway from Shildon to Darlington, and then on to Stockport, on 27 September 1825.

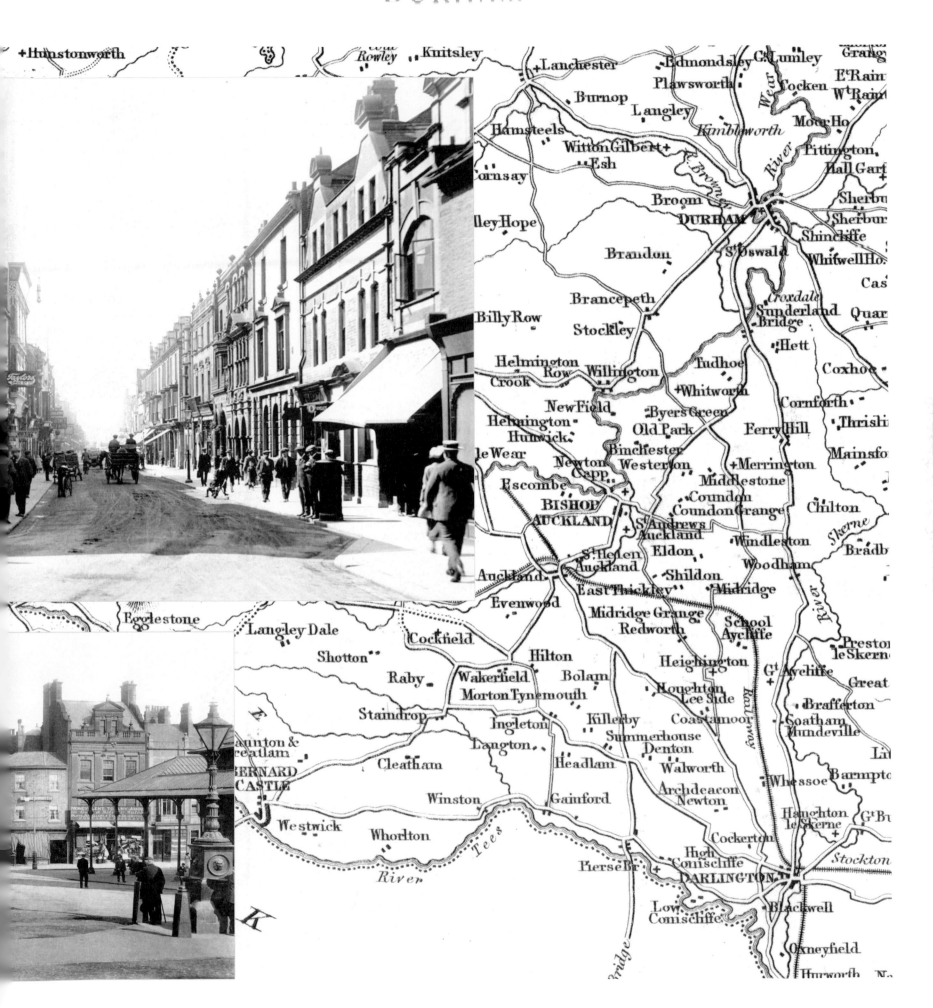

SOUTH SHIELDS c1898
S162005
At the time of this photograph South Shields had the largest number of seamen as a proportion of its population than anywhere else in Britain. However South Shields was not only a port, with ship-yards and ship repairers; it was also a colliery, with a pit almost in the town centre.

STOCKTON-ON-TEES, HIGH STREET 1899 44738
After the 'Locomotion' made her historic journey to Stockton, the town turned from a quiet market town into a busy industrial centre. The town's other claim to fame is as the birthplace of the furniture designer Thomas Sheraton (1751-1806).

northumberland

Known as the 'Cradle of Christianity' because of the connections with St Aidan and St Cuthbert, Northumberland has a strong religious history. The county has also seen many bloody raids and border battles, and is home not only to churches and monasteries but mighty castles, pele towers and, of course, Hadrian's Wall. Industry has also played a strong part in the shaping of the area. The Pennines were a source of lead. Deep mining for coal was once important; during the Industrial Revolution, Northumberland was the biggest supplier in the country, and the development of mines led to the growth of towns to accommodate the workers. Along the rugged coastline, fishing was once the livelihood of many, and fisher-folk followed the shoals of herring during their summer migration. Today, a large part of the country depends on agriculture, especially sheep farming, and forestry, with tourism of major importance to the local economy.

**CRASTER,
THE HARBOUR 1951**
C352001
About a mile from the harbour is the 15th-century Craster Tower that gave the village its name.

NEWCASTLE UPON TYNE, SWING BRIDGE 1890 N16018
Newcastle takes its name from the 'new castle' built by the Normans on the site of a Roman fort; it grew to be the commercial and industrial capital
of the north-east. When the late 18th-century bridge over the Tyne was demolished in the 1870s to make way for the Swing Bridge, traces of an earlier medieval
bridge (destroyed by floods in 1771) and a Roman bridge were discovered. The Swing Bridge cost £288,000 to build. It has an overall length of 560ft;
the swing section is 281ft, giving two navigable channels each 104ft wide.

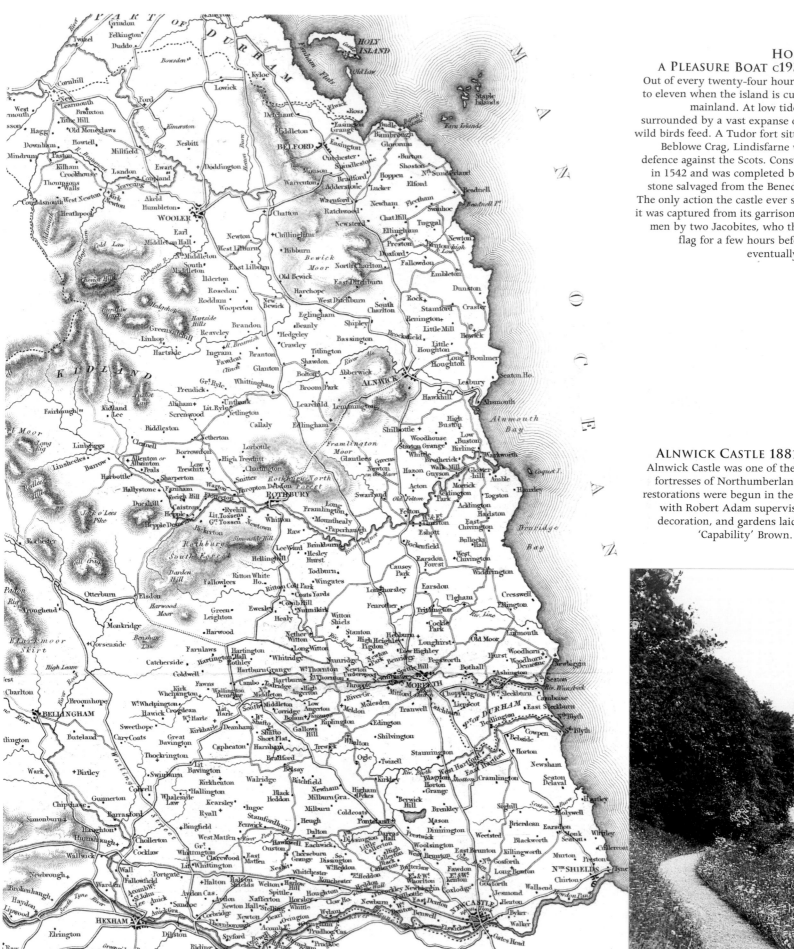

HOLY ISLAND, A PLEASURE BOAT c1935 H348133

Out of every twenty-four hours there are up to eleven when the island is cut off from the mainland. At low tide the island is surrounded by a vast expanse of sand where wild birds feed. A Tudor fort sitting on top of Beblowe Crag, Lindisfarne was raised for defence against the Scots. Constuction began in 1542 and was completed by 1550, using stone salvaged from the Benedictine Priory. The only action the castle ever saw was when it was captured from its garrison of just seven men by two Jacobites, who then flew their flag for a few hours before they were eventually thrown out.

ALNWICK CASTLE 1881 13973

Alnwick Castle was one of the five great fortresses of Northumberland. Major restorations were begun in the late 1700s, with Robert Adam supervising the decoration, and gardens laid out by 'Capability' Brown.

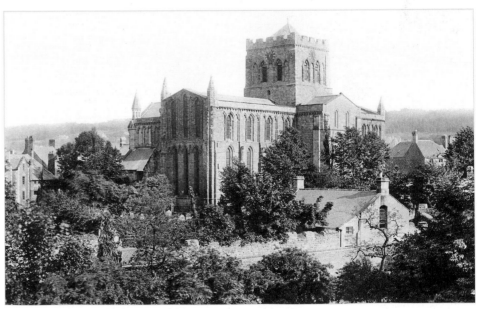

HEXHAM, THE ABBEY 1888 21062
The great abbey church of St Andrew is what makes Hexham important. The first church at Hexham was founded by St Wilfrid on land given him in AD674 by Queen Ethelreda of Northumbria. The present abbey dates from the 12th to the 15th centuries, though the crypt of St Wilfrid's original church remains.

NEWCASTLE UPON TYNE, THE QUAYSIDE 1928 N16016
The River Tyne is crossed by the great arch of Newcastle's suspension bridge, erected in 1928.

NEWCASTLE UPON TYNE, GRAINGER STREET 1900 N16014

Three men, Richard Grainger, John Dobson, and John Clayton were responsible for much of the centre of Newcastle. Grainger and Dobson supplied the architectural talent, and Clayton the money and influence. Dobson's porticoed Central Station in Newcastle is his masterpiece, a monument to the railway age that is most appropriate to Newcastle since the railway pioneer, George Stephenson, was born in the village of Wylam, 8 miles from the city.

INDEX

FREE PRINT OF YOUR CHOICE

Mounted Print
Overall size 14 x 11 inches (355 x 280mm)

Choose any Frith photograph in this book.
Simply complete the Voucher opposite and return it with your remittance for £2.25 (to cover postage and handling) and we will print the photograph of your choice in SEPIA (size 11 x 8 inches) and supply it in a cream mount with a burgundy rule line (overall size 14 x 11 inches).
Please note: photographs with a reference number starting with a "Z" are not Frith photographs and cannot be supplied under this offer.
Offer valid for delivery to UK addresses only.

PLUS: Order additional Mounted Prints at HALF PRICE - £7.49 each (normally £14.99)
If you would like to order more Frith prints from this book, possibly as gifts for friends and family, you can buy them at half price (with no additional postage and handling costs).

PLUS: Have your Mounted Prints framed
For an extra £14.95 per print you can have your mounted print(s) framed in an elegant polished wood and gilt moulding, overall size 16 x 13 inches (no additional postage and handling required).

IMPORTANT!

These special prices are only available if you use this form to order. You must use the ORIGINAL VOUCHER on this page (no copies permitted). We can only despatch to one address. This offer cannot be combined with any other offer.

Send completed Voucher form to:
The Francis Frith Collection, Frith's Barn, Teffont, Salisbury, Wiltshire SP3 5QP

CHOOSE A PHOTOGRAPH FROM THIS BOOK

Voucher for **FREE** and Reduced Price Frith Prints

Please do not photocopy this voucher. Only the original is valid, so please fill it in, cut it out and return it to us with your order.

Picture ref no	Page no	Qty	Mounted @ £7.49	Framed + £14.95	Total Cost
		1	Free of charge*	£	£
			£7.49	£	£
			£7.49	£	£
			£7.49	£	£
			£7.49	£	£
			£7.49	£	£

Please allow 28 days for delivery

* Post & handling (UK)	£2.25
Total Order Cost	£

Title of this book . . . .

I enclose a cheque/postal order for £ . . . . made payable to 'The Francis Frith Collection'

OR please debit my Mastercard / Visa / Switch (Maestro) /Amex card
(credit cards please on all overseas orders), details below

Card Number

Issue No (Switch only)   Valid from (Amex/Switch)

Expires   Signature

Name Mr/Mrs/Ms . . . .

Address . . . .

. . . .

. . . .

. . . . Postcode . . . .

Daytime Tel No . . . .

Email . . . .

Valid to 31/12/07